Any-3:

Anyone, Anywhere, Anytime

by Mike Shipman

Any-3: *Anyone, Anywhere, Anytime*

by Mike Shipman

WIGTake Resources
P.O. Box 1884
Monument, CO 80132
1 (719) 646-3190
www.churchplantingmovements.com
Printed in USA

Any-3: Anyone, Anywhere, Anytime
by Mike Shipman

WIGTake Resources,
P.O. Box 1884, Monument, CO 80132
1 (719) 646-3190
www.churchplantingmovements.com/bookstore

ISBN-13: 978-1-939124-00-5
1. Missions. 2. Church planting. 3. Discipleship.
Shipman, Michael, 1966 –

Printed by Bookmasters

Cover Design by Mike Mirabella

Page Design by Megan Chadwick

Shipman, Michael
    Any-3: Anyone, Anywhere, Anytime

CONTENTS

ACKNOWLEDGMENTS

WORDS CANNOT EXPRESS the glory of the gospel gift. I consider this book a tribute to the giver of the gift, Jesus Christ. If this book succeeds in equipping and motivating His servants to proclaim the gospel to others, then the Lord Jesus deserves all credit for initiating and guiding the Any-3 book.

Sincerest appreciation is due to my dear wife and our three children. Their sacrifices and contributions to this book are numerous. Their support has been unwavering and their insights invaluable.

Many people have influenced the Any-3 approach. Early in my ministry, Dr. C. Sumner Wemp modeled this kind of evangelism in restaurants, airplanes, and everywhere that he met lost people. During 27 years of Christian ministry, numerous mentors and co-workers have contributed by the ways they have lived out the Great Commission. The mental notes I've taken from their ministries have guided the way I view evangelism, resulting in Any-3.

My co-workers in the harvest field deserve acknowledgement. For the past fourteen years I've worked alongside inspiring men and women who have dedicated their lives to bringing the multitudes to saving faith. I'm continually learning from their experiences, as they share the gospel and train others to evangelize. I am deeply grateful for the many colleagues around the world who have read this manuscript in its draft stages, and offered invaluable suggestions, insights and corrections. I've tried to give credit in this book when the ideas expressed originated from others. Regrettably, it was often best not to mention individual names for security reasons, but rather they are cited simply as colleagues.

I owe special thanks to several supervisors and colleagues who opened doors for Any-3. Had they not believed in Any-3, it would never have been disseminated broadly. Todd L. and Brad R. gave me an opportunity to present Any-3 to a multi-regional audience. Mark S. introduced it to others and gave valuable input as Any-3 developed. Steve Smith, Neill M. and Keith M. have given me many opportunities to train Christian workers in various contexts. David Garrison deemed Any-3 worthy of publication, did the difficult task of editing, and made this book possible.

My utmost appreciation belongs to my heroes. They are the men and women from various nationalities who daily apply Any-3. They joyfully face ridicule and threats in order to make the Savior's sacrifice and resurrection known. May their example motivate us to proclaim the gospel to anyone, anywhere, and at any time.

Mike Shipman

Part One

ANY-3 BREAKTHROUGH

1
God at Work
in the Muslim World

I SLAM IS THE fastest growing religion in the world. But what if I were to tell you that in my country thousands of Muslims are now turning to the gospel, accepting Jesus Christ as Savior and Lord, and embracing a new life as His followers?

It's true. Over the past five years tens of thousands of Muslims around the world have given their lives to Jesus as Lord and Savior. In this book, you will travel into the middle of one of the fastest growing movements of Muslims to Christ. You will see just how and why more than 9,000 Muslims in one Southeast Asian country have said yes to Jesus, and been born again.[1] You will learn how more than 3,500 of these have been baptized into new churches that have reproduced themselves as many as eight and nine times, producing hundreds of fellowships of new believers.

Just as important, you will learn how you, too, can effectively bring Muslims to faith in Jesus Christ — *anyone, anywhere, anytime.*

---

[1] Because of its heavy reliance on the New Testament gospel, the Christology, or understanding of Christ's nature, in the Any-3 movements have typically been high. Christ is viewed as fully God, as well as fully man.

The Challenge of Islam

While it's true that Islam is the fastest growing religion in the world today, a closer look at that growth reveals why it is growing. The largest factor by far is biological reproduction. Not only are Muslim families producing more children than most of the societies around them, thanks to improvements in healthcare and living conditions, more of their children are growing up to raise families of their own. The result is a population explosion within the Muslim world that is spilling over into countries around the globe.

What this means for you is that you *will* face the growing reality of Islam. If you have not already, you will eventually find yourself with Muslim neighbors, classmates, or co-workers. In short, Christians today *will* encounter Islam. The question is, will we encounter it well, or poorly?

The truth is, Islam is the only major religion in the world that was custom designed to contest and confound the Christian faith. The resulting religion has many anti-Christian components within it. It's small wonder that unprepared Christians today so often find it intimidating.

Given this very real challenge, many well-intentioned Christians have responded with fear and anger. However, reactions stemming from fear and anger seldom achieve what God desires. What God desires is that all Muslims would know Him and the good news of salvation that He offers in Jesus Christ.

This is God's day of salvation for Muslims. Wouldn't it be tragic if we missed it, because we were too afraid of Muslims or too busy fighting against them to introduce them to Christ?

Dear friend in Christ, we must open our eyes to see that this is God's day of salvation for Muslims, *but only if we are prepared for the harvest!* Any-3 can help to prepare and equip you for that harvest.

The Any-3 Breakthrough

Seven years ago, Zack and I were in over our heads. We had accepted the challenge of engaging a large Muslim unreached people group with the gospel.[2] Out of our frustration and failures, we desperately sought the Lord in prayer. It was through this process that God led us to develop a new discipleship initiative aimed at multiplying personal evangelism, new disciples and new churches.

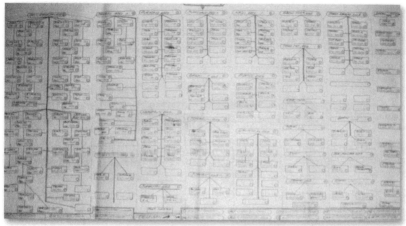

Nine Generations of Muslim-Background Churches

Zack and I made a conscious commitment to share the gospel with anyone we met, anywhere, and at any time. For this reason, we called our strategy "Any-3." Our first breakthrough came one day when Zack shared the gospel with a man in line with him at a public office. To our delight, the man soon afterward professed faith in Christ. But Any-3 is more than just a commitment to share the gospel; it is a way of sharing that is proving effective in unlocking peoples' willingness to say yes to Jesus.

---

[2] All of the stories in this book are true, but the names have been changed to protect the ministries of those involved. The graphic <Nine Generations of Muslim-Background Churches> originally appeared in Steve Smith's *T4T: A Discipleship Re-Revolution* (Monument, CO: WIGTake Resources, 2011), p. 118, but it was about our Any-3 movement, which incorporates T4T in its follow-up program (see Chapter 14 below).

Seven years after that first convert, more than 5,000 Muslims from the people group with whom we serve have professed faith in Jesus Christ through Any-3 style evangelism. We are seeing believers and churches reproduce in multiplying generations. Of the more than 450 groups that have formed among our people group, one-third of them are fourth generation and beyond.[3] Any-3 evangelism has become our primary evangelism method for the growing church-planting movement[4] in our ministry. The reason for this is not because of some magical formula within Any-3, but because Any-3 provides us with a way to simply and effectively present the gospel to Muslims and gather them into discipling communities. The power is in the gospel, not the method. The method is just the vehicle for presenting that powerful gospel.

Any-3 is proving to be an effective tool for both Western and non-Western Christian witnesses. It is helping hundreds of professional Christian workers and thousands of ordinary Christians get over their fear of sharing the gospel with Muslims. Recently, a Christian worker who had failed again and again as he tried to evangelize his people group was introduced to Any-3. Soon after, he sent the author a text message in all capitals, "I'M SHARING THE GOSPEL!" Indeed he was sharing and more; now he and his friends are leading Muslims to Christ on a weekly basis in the same difficult area where they had formerly faced frustration. Any-3 has rejuvenated his ministry.

A missionary in Asia named Marcus had experienced some success in his difficult Muslim unreached people group. But now, using Any-3, he was seeing a breakthrough. Marcus reported, "We have baptized more people in our people group in the past six months than we did in the previous five years combined."

---

[3] By fourth generation, we mean one church that has reproduced itself, and that church has reproduced itself, and that church has reproduced itself, and that church has reproduced itself, thus four generations of reproduction. Generational data cited here was last measured in the first quarter of 2009.

[4] Church Planting Movements are described at length in David Garrison's book, *Church Planting Movements, How God Is Redeeming a Lost World* (Richmond: WIGTake Resources, 2004).

This book is built on biblical research, and trial and error in mentoring evangelists in productive evangelism approaches. When you, the reader, digest the contents of this book, we believe you will conclude, "This is a clear, biblical yet culturally appropriate way of sharing the gospel. This could work in my own community."

This is harvest time. God is preparing the fields and raising up thousands of harvesters throughout the world to reach the lost for Jesus Christ. As you will see, the basic Any-3 principles that have proven so effective within the Muslim world, have implications for reaching Hindus, Buddhists, and even Christian background persons as well.

Why Any-3?

What makes Any-3 different from other contemporary evangelism methods? Any-3 implements the simple, natural way Jesus witnessed to the woman at the well in John 4. In so doing, it recaptures foundational elements of first-century evangelism that Jesus modeled for His disciples. It worked then, and it works now.

Any-3 combines bridging, gospel presentation and drawing the net into one seamless approach. Now it is once again easy to transition from small talk to the gospel, and then bring the conversation to a decision. Any-3 allows you to share the gospel in a natural and relational manner. It is persuasive, but never combative. In this way, Any-3 unleashes the power of the gospel without provoking the ire of the listener.

Any-3 trains the witness how to get to a gospel conversation naturally, by answering the question, "What do I say to a non-Christian?" Any-3 helps witnessing become relational, rather than preachy. This empowers the witness to become competent and confident as he navigates the obstacles that typically arise in a witnessing conversation.

Any-3 doesn't have a "packaged" feel to it. It feels spontaneous and free, helping Christians live an evangelizing lifestyle, rather than try in vain to do lifestyle evangelism.

By using the gospel itself as a filter, Any-3 immediately reveals who is and is not open to the gospel. So, instead of having to guess how a person might respond to the gospel based on body language or some other subjective factor, Any-3 lets you know for certain.

We are doing today what very few people dreamed could be done among Muslims – sharing the gospel and often hearing them say, "Thank you." Even when they don't say, "Thank you," they generally listen to the gospel, and show respect to the messenger of good news.

Pushing the limits beyond what we thought was possible, we have found that we can share the gospel with almost anyone, almost anywhere, at almost any time with surprisingly little opposition -- even in our high security Muslim context. Sharing the gospel with Any-3 has yielded similar results for those we have trained. Yes, when people profess faith and follow Christ in baptism, persecution does arise, as it has since Pentecost. However, because of the effectiveness of Any-3, by the time the persecution comes, there is a growing community of believers to weather the storm together.

Because its principles derive from the evangelism pattern modeled by Jesus, Any-3 can be adapted to virtually any culture or worldview. This book will focus on the Muslim world, arguably one of the toughest to reach, because that is where we have seen for ourselves just how effective Any-3 is. However, as you will learn in the final part of this book, with slight adjustments, Any-3 can be adapted to other worldviews and cultures as well.

God is using Any-3 to awaken and empower His people to joyfully share the gospel once again. Those who do are experiencing for themselves the gospel's power and joy. In the pages that follow, I invite you to see for yourself how God can use Any-3 to glorify His name among the nations, and perhaps even in your own ministry.

2
A Five-Step Journey

THIS CHAPTER UNVEILS the heart of Any-3. You will begin to learn, step by step, how to progress from first time encounter to a decision for Christ. In the chapter that follows, Chapter Three, we will explore the biblical foundation for Any-3, as we examine the pattern set out by Jesus in his witnessing encounter with the woman at the well. But first, let's see Any-3 in action, and learn the five simple steps for witnessing.

Derek was tired, it had been a long day, but he was determined to share the gospel one more time before retiring for the night. As he walked through a secluded area of a conservative Muslim suburb, he prayed for the Lord to connect him with someone with whom he could share the gospel.

Hasan was sitting at a small food-stall drinking juice as Derek passed by. Hasan was waiting for his wife, who was in a salon. Seeing Hasan, Derek purchased a drink as well, and sat down near him.

"Hello" Derek said. "Good evening." Hasan replied.[5] The two soon began making small talk as they passed the time.

---

[5] With Muslims, a common opening greeting is "*Salaam aleikum*" which literally means, "Peace be upon you." I have translated the greeting we use in my country into the more familiar English-language "Hello" or "Good evening."

Quite naturally, Derek asked Hasan about his religion. The conversation maintained a relaxed tone, but Derek knew where he wanted it to go. With a few casual questions by Derek, the two agreed that mankind shared a common sin problem. Hasan agreed, "Yes, we're all sinners."

Derek asked Hasan what he was doing to get his sins forgiven. Hasan mentioned three of the five activities his religion requires to please God. Then Hasan admitted, "My sins aren't forgiven yet, I don't know when they'll be forgiven. On the judgment day, I can only hope my sins will be forgiven." Derek was expecting this answer, knowing that Muslims rarely have any assurance of their own salvation.

Derek then politely, yet confidently, told Hasan that he knew his own sins were forgiven. He then explained how he knew, by telling Hasan a story. Over the next few minutes, Derek shared with Hasan a story emphasizing that Christ is God's sacrificial Lamb, who died for our sins and was raised from the dead. Derek concluded by telling Hasan that anyone who surrenders himself to Jesus with repentance of sin and belief in the gospel, will have his sins forgiven.

Hasan responded by agreeing with Derek. It made sense to him that his good works could never cancel out all of his sins, but that God had made a way for forgiveness through Jesus. When Derek asked Hasan if he believed the gospel, Hasan replied with words of sincere conviction and openness. He was convinced that what Derek had shared was true, even though this was the first time he had heard the good news about Jesus' sacrifice for him.

Derek then quoted Romans 10:9, explaining the need for repentance and surrender to Jesus Christ as Lord. That same night, Hasan believed that God was calling him to salvation and prayed to surrender himself to Jesus. Hasan responded to the gospel, and Derek's evangelistic zeal was renewed.[6]

---

[6] Although some persons profess faith during the initial conversation, when they first hear the gospel, it is more common for them to profess faith during the first, second, or third follow-up visits.

We often experience encounters like this as we share the gospel. Some people obviously aren't as open as Hasan, and they politely bow out of the conversation, but usually not until after hearing the gospel. Many others, though, respond just as Hasan did.

This is Any-3. Any-3 is an intentional path for sharing with Muslims that flows smoothly yet systematically from initial connection to decision for Christ. A review of the witnessing encounter with Hasan will reveal how it flowed naturally and easily through each of the five steps. Later, we will see that these same five steps were evident in Jesus' evangelizing ministry as well. But first, let's take a look at these five steps.

ANY-3 AT A GLANCE

Step One: Get Connected

1. You can accomplish this with anyone by using two connecting questions: "Who are you?" and "How are you?"
2. Take time to get acquainted with them, their family. Be friendly and open.

Transition #1: "Are you Hindu, Muslim, Buddhist, or Christian?"

Step Two: Get to God

Step Two is accomplished with a question and an observation. The step two question is: "Most religions are alike, aren't they?" Then make the observation: "We are all trying to please God, so we can go to heaven some day, and we are all trying to pay off our sin debt. We all sin, don't we? Even good people sin. Sinning is easy, but paying off our sin debt to God is much more difficult, isn't it?"

Transition #2: "In your religion, what are you doing to get your sins forgiven?"

Step Three: Get to Lostness

After asking the person what are some of the things they are doing in their religion to please God and get their sins forgiven, let them tell you two or three things they are doing. Listen attentively and don't be afraid to ask questions along the way.

Wrap up the section by asking them three questions: First, "Are your sins paid off yet?" Second, "When do you think your sins will be paid off?" Third, "On Judgment Day, do you know that your sin debt will be paid?"

Transition #3: "What I believe is different; I know that my sins are forgiven. It is not because I am a good person, although I do try. I know my sins are forgiven, because God himself has made a way for our sins to be forgiven."

Step Four: Get to the Gospel

Tell *The First and Last Sacrifice Story* (see Chapter Six). Finish *The First and Last Sacrifice Story* by saying, "And that is why I know my sins are forgiven."

Transition #4: "According to the Bible, if we surrender our life to Jesus as Lord and believe that He has paid for our sins through His sacrifice and that God has raised Him from the dead, our sins will be forgiven."

Step Five: Get to a Decision

To bring your conversation to a decision, ask two questions. First, "That makes sense, doesn't it?" Though we cannot pay off our own sin debt, God has made a way for our sins to be forgiven through Jesus' sacrificial death and resurrection. Second, "Do you believe what I have told you: that Jesus died for our sins and was raised again?"[7]

Simple enough? Any-3 provides a direct path, guiding you from initial connection to presenting a clear and compelling

---

[7] If the person responds affirmatively to this question, the next step would be to read Romans 10:9-10 together, stressing the need for them to repent of sin and surrender to Christ as Lord. The entire follow-up process is described in Chapter Ten.

invitation to follow Jesus Christ. We'll look more closely at each of the five steps in subsequent chapters. For now, though, take a moment to commit to memory each of the five steps.

Capture What You've Learned:
The Five Steps of Any-3

Get Connected

Get to God

Get to Lostness

Get to the Gospel

Get to a Decision

3
Witnessing Well

J **ESUS IS OUR** model for everything in the Christian life, including how to do evangelism. Yet detailed accounts of Jesus' witnessing are limited. We find the most complete and instructive insight into Jesus' pattern of witnessing in John 4, where Jesus shared the gospel with a Samaritan woman beside a well.

To be certain, a mixed-race woman, with a reputation for immorality, made for an interesting case study. In witnessing to her Jesus overcame social taboos of his day. Jewish men normally avoided contact with both Samaritans and women. Conventional wisdom said, "No man should hold a conversation with a female along the way, in fact not even with his own wife."[8] Jesus would have known the rabbinic opinion that, "It is better to burn the words of the Mosaic Law, rather than teach them to a female."[9]

Perhaps Jesus chose such an extreme example to make a point. We must be ready to share the gospel with anyone and at any time. That is the nature of Any-3; it equips you to share

---

[8] Cited by Barclay, *Gospel of John*, vol. 1, 155 in Elmer Towns, *The Gospel of John: Believe and Live* (Old Tappan, NJ: Fleming and Revell Co., 1990), 101.

[9] Elmer Towns, *The Gospel of John: Believe and Live* (Old Tappan, NJ: Fleming and Revell Co., 1990), 101.

with anyone, anywhere and at any time. Beside the well, Jesus brought the principles of Any-3 evangelism to life.

Through his conversation with the woman at the well, Jesus revealed to his followers, then and now, important time-tested principles about how to share the gospel. The following pages will show you how we can apply these same principles today. Any-3 prepares us to always be ready to witness well, just as Jesus did at the well.

Jesus was traveling with His disciples from Judea to Galilee (John 4:3). To get to Galilee, the Bible says, Jesus *had* to pass through Samaria (John 4:4). From a practical standpoint, though, Jesus did not *have* to pass through Samaria. If Jesus had been in a hurry He might have chosen to pass through Samaria, because the road through Samaria was more direct, and therefore faster. However, Jesus was not in a hurry. We know this because Jesus and His disciples stayed in Samaria for two days after his encounter with the woman at the well (John 4:43). Jesus *had* to pass through Samaria, to obey the will of His Father. Witnessing well begins with obedience to the Holy Spirit's leadership.

HOW DID JESUS WITNESS AT THE WELL?

Step One: Jesus Connected
Established commonality

The first thing Jesus did was to make a connection with the woman. Jesus said, "Give Me a drink" (John 4:7). The request is interesting because of its directness. If there was an introductory greeting or conversation, it is not recorded by John. Normally, any witnessing conversation would begin with small talk about where the person's family is from, where the person lives, the weather, current events, etc. This may have happened although it is not recorded.

"Give me a drink" provided an immediate relational bridge drawing on the common ground between the two persons. With this request, Jesus and the woman, though from very differing backgrounds, could meet on common territory. It also connected them with the frustration of having to come to the well from a considerable distance to draw water. Finding common ground is the first objective in developing a witnessing conversation.

Jesus' witnessing encounter by the well dispels a common myth: that a relationship or friendship has to exist for the witness to succeed. In fact, the woman herself recognized the vast difference between herself and Jesus. She said, "How is it that You, being a Jew, ask me for a drink since I am a Samaritan woman" (John 4:9)? Nevertheless, Jesus found a simple commonality - thirst. Jesus and the woman shared common human aspirations and needs.

Jesus also dispelled another witnessing myth: that it takes time to build up the sort of relationship that would allow a person to hear the gospel. Jesus initiated a conversation with the Samaritan woman, and within minutes (if not seconds) was already into a conversation about spiritual matters.

Step Two: Jesus Got to a God Conversation
Transitioned to spiritual matters

Once Jesus had connected with the Samaritan woman, he quickly transitioned to spiritual matters. Jesus' short bridge is impressive. The conversation centered on a common need, and then quickly bridged into a discussion about the Living Water.

Jesus said, "If you knew the gift of God, and who it is who says to you, 'Give Me a drink,' you would have asked Him, and He would have given you Living Water." Jesus used the analogy of Living Water to raise interest in spiritual matters and left the woman wanting to know more.

Step Three: Jesus Got to Lostness
Led her to see her own lostness

Jesus revealed the heart of the woman's problem in order to reveal its cure. Jesus would not let the woman ignore her sin, or find the cure without addressing what had created her spiritual thirst. The woman had to acknowledge her sinfulness in order to be cured of its consequences.

Jesus did not immediately grant her request to, "Give me this water" (John 4:15b). Instead, in verse 16, He said, "Go, call your husband and come here." When she tried to avoid the subject by replying, "I have no husband." Jesus said, "...you have had five husbands, and the one whom you now have is not your husband; this you have said truly." Ouch! Jesus could have just as easily told the woman to call her friends, but he chose instead to help her see her lost and sinful condition.

At this point in the witnessing conversation, Jesus' approach differs from our own. As the sinless Son of God, Jesus could not personally identify with the sinfulness of the woman at the well. One thing we can say when we witness, that Jesus couldn't say is:, "We, too, are sinners." We can agree with the person with whom we are witnessing that sin is the universal problem of all mankind.

Like Jesus, we should not avoid the topic of sin and its consequences, nor should we communicate a "holier than thou" attitude. Discussing sin and separation from God usually builds a stronger bond between the witness and the hearer. We are in the same sinking boat. Though we often see commonality in our shared interests, our greatest bond is found in the shared problem of sin and its devastating effects in our lives.

Always remember, though, it's not our job to convict a person of lostness. That is the Holy Spirit's job. "And He, when He comes, will convict the world concerning sin, and righteousness and judgment; concerning sin, because they do not believe in Me; and concerning righteousness, because I go to the Father and you no longer see Me; and concerning judgment, because the ruler of this world has been judged" (John 16:8-11).

Any-3 is particularly effective with Muslims, because it invites them to admit their own lostness. Then, with the Holy Spirit's prompting, they are prepared to accept the solution that God has provided in the sacrificial atonement of Jesus Christ. When a Christian directs the conversation toward our mutual sinfulness and its cure, he works in partnership with the Holy Spirit to raise awareness of our need for a savior.

Step Four: Jesus Got to the Gospel
Proclaimed Himself as the Messiah

Meanwhile, back at the well, Jesus was drawing a distinction between the woman's religious practices and the true way of salvation. He acknowledged the religious differences between Samaritans and Jews, but then pointed her to true worship.

The conversation went as follows:

Our fathers worshipped in this mountain, and you people say that in Jerusalem is the place where men ought to worship." Jesus said to her, "Woman, believe Me, an hour is coming when neither in this mountain nor in Jerusalem will you worship the Father. You worship what you do not know; we worship what we know, for salvation is from the Jews. But an hour is coming, and now is, when the true worshippers will worship the Father in spirit and truth; for such people the Father seeks to be His worshippers. God is spirit, and those who worship Him must worship in spirit and truth. (John 4:20-24)

According to Jesus, the point was not where a person worshipped, but that worship be grounded in truth and in spirit, because God is spirit.

After agreeing on the problem of universal and personal sinfulness, Jesus transitioned the conversation to the solution. Where does salvation come from? Jesus answered the question by announcing that He was the Messiah (verse 26).

Almost every religion presupposes that mankind must do something to repair a broken or imperfect relationship with God. The solutions they propose are typically works-based ways to repair that separation between God and man.

In Buddhism, salvation is pursued through emptying oneself of all desire in pursuit of Nirvana. In Hinduism, salvation is accomplished through becoming "one" with all things. In Islam, people *may* be saved through keeping the five pillars:

Saying the Muslim confession of faith – "There is no God but Allah, and Mohammad is his messenger," saying prayers five times daily in Arabic while bowing toward Mecca, giving alms, fasting during the month of Ramadan, and taking the pilgrimage to Mecca. Other religions present their own ways to gain favor and salvation from God.

The Bible reveals a different way from all the rest. Many Christians have also missed this point, placing their hope of salvation upon their good works. What the Bible teaches, though, is that salvation is a gift of God that comes through faith in the sacrifice of Jesus Christ who paid mankind's debt of sin with His sacrificial death.

When we witness, we must differentiate between attempting salvation through our own works and salvation through the work of God in Jesus Christ. Jesus said, "If you knew the gift of God...He would have given you Living Water" (John 4:10). Salvation is not earned; it is a gift from God.

Step Five: Jesus Got to a Decision
Invited her to receive His message and arranged follow-up

Had the woman not been open to Jesus' message, we assume that He would have heeded his own advice to his disciples, "Any place that does not receive you or listen to you, as you go out from there, shake the dust off the soles of your feet for a testimony against them" (Mark 6:11). However, the woman was very open, and Jesus led her to faith. John's Gospel tells us that Jesus remained in the area for two days of follow-up.

Drawing the Net
Unless a person says that he or she is not interested, you should call for a decision by asking, "Do you believe what I've told you (the gospel)?" This is the only true indicator of their level of openness. Many persons will be interested in Christ the first time they hear the gospel. Perhaps the person has heard the gospel before, or perhaps God has prepared his heart. The only way to know for sure is to ask.

In the past, I rarely asked anyone if he believed the gospel if he said it was the first time he had heard it. I thought he could only progress by one or two "stair steps." Now I understand that when the Lord is drawing someone to salvation, He often uses an elevator rather than stairs. He can take them almost simultaneously from never having heard the gospel to genuine saving faith. So, unless the person has said that he is rejecting the gospel, ask him if he believes it.

Arranging Follow-Up

You should try to revisit responsive persons within 48 hours of the initial conversation. Jesus warned us that when new believers are left alone to consider the gospel, Satan will try to turn them away. Like a bird plucking a seed from the field, before it has a chance to take root, Satan will try to snatch the gospel seed out of their heart (Luke 8:5).

Follow-up was the key for solidifying the faith of the Samaritan woman and for reaching many others through her. Jesus' desire for reaching beyond the woman at the well was evident early on in the witnessing conversation. "Go, call your husband and come here" (John 4:16) is a clear indication that Jesus was attempting to draw a group of people, rather than a single individual to faith. Upon showing openness to Christ's message, the woman went into the city and invited several men to "come, see a man who told me all the things that I have done; this is not the Christ, is it" (John 4:29)? The woman's question, although stated negatively, was hopeful that, in fact, Jesus was the Messiah. Jesus stayed there two days with the result that, "Many more believed because of His word" (John 4:41).

You will find a thorough presentation of how to do Any-3 follow-up in Chapter Fourteen, "Follow-up for a CPM (Church Planting Movement)." If you follow the suggested pattern in that chapter, you just might find that you've launched a church-planting movement.

If Any-3 really does follow the evangelism pattern modeled by Jesus with the Samaritan woman, then we should expect to see this same pattern followed by the New Testament disciples of Jesus as well. Reviewing evangelism in the book of Acts, this is exactly what we find.

ANY-3 IN THE ACTS OF THE EARLY CHURCH

Any-3 Parallels in the Book of Acts[10]

Witnessing in Acts mirrored the same basic pattern Jesus followed in John 4:1-42. In Acts 2:14-41; 3:12-26; 10:34-48; and 13:16-43 we find extensive records of evangelistic encounters. Each incident reveals the same five steps of the Any-3 process: 1) the witness made a connection, 2) a transition to a God conversation followed by a reference to 3) the hearer's sinfulness, leading to 4) a gospel presentation, and 5) an appeal to respond.

In each of the Acts passages, the witness proclaimed that Jesus died for people's sins and rose again, as foretold in prophecies and/or confirmed by witnesses. Those hearing the message were assured that a response to the gospel through faith and repentance would result in forgiveness of sins. Jesus was always presented as Christ (Savior) and often as Lord and coming Judge.

The principles of Any-3 are effective today, just as they were in the New Testament book of Acts, precisely because they originate with the patterns established by Jesus with a lost woman beside a well in Samaria. The following table shows the similarities between how the gospel was shared in Acts, compared with the Any-3 pattern.

---

[10] My colleague, Mark S., identified these characteristic patterns of witnessing in the book of Acts even before he was introduced to Any-3. After learning Any-3, Mark noticed the similarities, and shared these observations with me.

ACTS PATTERN	ANY-3 PATTERN
"Fellow Jews...."(Acts 2:14) "Men of Israel...." (Acts 3:12)	Step One: Get Connected
"These men are not drunk....this is what was spoken by the prophet Joel...." (Acts 2:15-16) "The God of Abraham ... has glorified his servant Jesus." (Acts 3:13)	Step Two: Get to God
"...You, with the help of wicked men, put him to death...."(Acts 2:23) "...They were cut to the heart." (Acts 2:37) "You handed him over to be killed, and you disowned him." (Acts 3:13-14)	Step Three: Get to Lostness
"...But God raised him from the dead." (Acts 2:22-24) "...You killed the author of life, but God raised him from the dead...." (Acts 3:13-16)	Step Four: Get to the Gospel
"Repent and be baptized, everyone of you...." (Acts 2:28) "Repent, then, and turn to God, so that your sins may be wiped out...." (Acts 3:18-20)	Step Five: Get to a Decision

4
Witnessing Well To Muslims

ANY-3 FOLLOWS THE approach that Jesus modeled with the Samaritan woman, the same pattern we commonly find in the book of Acts, and adapts it for witnessing to Muslims. The following section provides you with a more complete description of the five steps of Any-3.

FIVE STEPS TO WITNESSING WELL

Step One: Get Connected
Build rapport through friendly conversation

We get connected with two questions, "How are you?" and, "Who are you?" Enjoy getting to know the person before moving on to spiritual matters. Relax, interact with them about life, get acquainted with them by asking how they are doing.

For some, building rapport may take 3-7 minutes; others may spend 10-15 minutes. Establishing rapport is very important before you engage in witnessing.

Step Two: Get to God
Transition to spiritual matters

The purpose of "Getting to God" is to transition the conversation to spiritual matters and begin to establish that we are all sinners.

The Any-3 bridge for "Getting to God" is simple. Of course you'll want to pray for an open door to share the gospel, but even if the door does not appear open, go ahead and open it. Remember, we are not commanded to pray for a door to open, we are commanded to proclaim the gospel (Mark 16:15). So, pray for an open door, and use the following questions to help you get into a conversation about God.

Begin by asking: "What is your religion? Are you Hindu, Muslim, Buddhist or Christian?" After this question, make the observation: "Most religions are a like aren't they? We are all trying to please God, so we can go to heaven some day, and we are all trying to pay off our sin debt. We all sin, don't we? Even good people sin. Sinning is easy, but paying off our sin debt to God is much more difficult, isn't it?"

Step Three: Get to Lostness

Establish our common sin problem and the frustration of failing in our religious duties by letting them talk about their religious experience

Getting people to admit lostness sounds complicated, but it is remarkably easy. Most religious people are doing religious activities to pay off their sin debt. Therefore, we ask them, "In your religion, what are you doing to pay off your sin debt?"[11]

At this point, it's good to let them talk. Each time the person answers with something he is doing to pay off his debt to God, ask further about it. Once the person has discussed what he or she is doing to pay off his or her sin debt, use these three admission questions to transition to the next step:

THREE ADMISSION QUESTIONS

1. Is your sin debt paid off yet?

---

[11] Any-3 intentionally uses the analogy of "paying off a sin debt" because it sharpens the contrast between a Christian's assurance of salvation through the atoning work of Christ, and the Muslim's uncertainty about his eternal destiny.

2. When will it be paid off?

3. On Judgment Day, will your sins be forgiven?

Now that you have gotten connected, gotten to a God conversation, and led your Muslim friend to admit to lostness, you can get to the gospel with a transition statement like the following, "What I believe is different. I know my sins are forgiven, but not because I am a good person, even though I do try to be good. My sins are forgiven because God Himself has paid for my sins." Then, share *The First and Last Sacrifice Story* found in Chapter Six.[12]

Step Four: Get to the Gospel
Take 6-8 minutes to relate The First and Last Sacrifice Story

The First and Last Sacrifice Story is the way we share the gospel with Muslims in Any-3. We tell the gospel story rather than merely reciting propositional truths about the gospel.

Follow *The First and Last Sacrifice Story* with this transition question: "It makes sense, doesn't it, that we cannot pay off our own sins but that God made a way for our sins to be forgiven through Jesus' sacrifice?" and "Do you believe that Jesus died as a sacrifice for our sins and was raised from the dead?"

Step Five: Get to a Decision
After asking these transition questions, anticipate one of three possible responses:

1. They may believe the gospel.

2. They may be open to the gospel, but not yet ready to profess faith in Christ.

---

[12] One can make slight changes in this story when witnessing to a person of a different faith. These changes are suggested in Chapter Twelve. I have divided the story into three parts to make it easier to learn and use.

3. They may not yet believe the gospel.

Be prepared for each one of these responses with the following:

1. If they believe the gospel:

    Explain Romans 10:9-10, emphasizing the need to surrender to Christ as Lord through repentance and believing the gospel, "if you confess with your mouth Jesus as Lord, and believe in your heart that God raised Him from the dead, you shall be saved; for with the heart a person believes, resulting in righteousness, and with the mouth he confesses, resulting in salvation" (Romans 10:9-10).

    Now lead them in a prayer to surrender their life to Christ as Lord.

2. If they are open to the gospel, but not yet ready to profess faith:

    Briefly tell them one of the other Old Testament sacrifice stories (such as Cain and Abel) provided in Appendix A below. Emphasize the kind of sacrifice that God requires. Invite them to meet with you again to study other sacrifice stories from the Bible. Offer to pray for them in Jesus' name.

3. If they are not open to the gospel:

    Summarize the gospel again briefly, emphasizing the difference between the gospel and their religious activities aimed at paying off their sin debt to God. Then, feel free to politely change the subject or move on. You have faithfully planted a gospel seed that may yet yield a harvest after you are gone.

STICKING POINTS

Satan is constantly at work trying to prevent evangelism from succeeding. He "has blinded the minds of the unbelieving" (2 Corinthians 4:4), and they have "been held captive by him to do his will" (2 Timothy 2:26). Satan also uses deception to try to stop the witness. Anyone who has shared the gospel hears the deceiver's voice trying desperately to talk the witness out of sharing the good news. As long as the conversation is not about the gospel, there is no tension, but when the witness transitions to spiritual truth, the battle with Satan is on.

When a witness sets out to share the gospel, Satan will offer many opportunities for him to back out. Typically, there are three sticking points where the witness feels pressure to stop. These are critical points where the witness must submit himself to the Spirit of Christ and press on in order to effectively share the gospel.

The first sticking point comes when the witness transitions from small talk to spiritual truth, the voices start flowing. "Not now, not here, not so directly" are examples of frequent darts that are fired our way. Do not get stuck in mere small talk, because the huge issue of eternal life is at stake.

The second sticking point comes once we have worked with the Holy Spirit to get someone to understand and admit his lostness. Now it is time to transition to the gospel by stating, "What I believe is different…." At the same time, we hear the Liar's voice again saying, "Not too quickly, not so abruptly, not so clearly…You will surely offend them, and they will be turned off from you and the gospel…."

The third sticking point comes when it is time to draw the net. We have learned that you will never know if they believe the gospel until you ask them. This final question is the filter that shows whether the person is ready to believe, open to the gospel, or not yet open. By asking, "Do you believe what I have shared with you?" you open the door for immediate follow up, which could result in their profession of faith, baptism and discipleship.

Do not leave them in their lostness — give them the good news that can save them for eternity!

When Christians walk in the Spirit, share the gospel, and draw the net, people of all kinds are showing openness and coming to faith. Early in the movement that we have been a part of, two of the converts shared their amazement when a Muslim man, who had already been to Mecca for the pilgrimage, professed faith in Christ during their first encounter with him. "We simply shared the gospel, and then invited him to receive Christ," he said, "And he did!"

Three Sticking Points

1. When you transition from small talk to spiritual conversation.

2. When you make the transition statement: "What I believe is different."

3. When you draw the net by asking, "Do you believe what I have told you about Jesus' sacrificial death for our sins?"

Part Two
BRIDGES AND BEE STINGS

5
Bridging to a God Conversation

TRANSITIONING A CONVERSATION from small talk to God is difficult for many people. They don't quite know what to say, and they reluctantly go to a God conversation because they expect the conversation to become tense and uncomfortable. One of the many surprises for people we train is that it becomes as natural to talk about God as about family and friends.

In order to begin talking about spiritual matters, we ask people about their religion in a non-threatening way. Knowing almost certainly that the person with whom I'm conversing is Muslim, I ask him, "Are you a Hindu, Muslim, Buddhist or Christian?"

If I know he's a Muslim, ask if he's a Hindu. First, by giving another choice first, the question doesn't sound as threatening as if I were to say, "You're a Muslim, aren't you?" Second, there are some Hindus in our area. Therefore, be sure to include options from religions that are actually present in your area.

We follow up the question about the person's religion by making a statement about the similarities between most religions. Notice that I do not say, "All religions are alike"; I say, "Most religions are alike, aren't they?" Almost all religions are alike, because they reveal mankind's attempt to get to God by doing good or religious activities. Another way to say practically the same thing is, "There are many similarities between our religions, aren't there?"

The Any-3 bridge is ironic for me, because it takes advantage of the very phrase I used to dread. Early in our career overseas the phrase, "All religions are alike," extinguished many productive spiritual conversations. Now I've learned to use that phrase to bridge into a God conversation.

Using a statement about the similarities of religions builds a bridge instead of a wall. Finding something to agree upon is a good starting point for a conversation. By starting with, "Most religions are alike," we will have a chance a few minutes later to say, "What I believe is different," and to tell the gospel story.

After saying that most religions are alike, we point out two similarities. First, we're all trying to please God. Second, we're all trying to get our sins paid off or forgiven. We emphasize the second point, because this gives us an opportunity to discuss that we're all sinners and the impossibility of paying off our own sins.

"Most religions are alike," is the statement we make to open up a God conversation. Don't get caught up on comparing religions! Don't spend long on the bridge, just make the comment and then begin talking about sin.

Too often, the witness brings tension into the conversation as he attempts to transition to a God conversation. People experience breakthroughs in witnessing when they can begin talking about God with the same relaxed tone as though they are speaking of every-day things. Later in the conversation the hearer of the gospel may experience an inner struggle, because of the Holy Spirit's conviction. This need not be the case for the witness, though, as he confidently guides the conversation from small talk to God, the gospel, and a decision.

Variations

The religion question is proving to be a natural bridge to a God conversation with Muslims in pluralistic societies, and actually strengthens the connection between the witness and the other person. In societies where there is only one legal religion, the witness may bypass the religion question, beginning discussion with the fact that we're all sinners. This is logically followed by the question, "What are you doing to pay off your sins?"

Can local believers use the same bridge, even though they should know the hearer's religious preference? Interestingly, many local Christians do use the same bridge, particularly when they go to areas where they are not already recognized as a local. They like the indirectness of the question and how it frames the gospel conversation. With persons they know, some local believers replace the question with a different question such as, "Have you said your prayers yet?" or "Have you given alms today?" This question is followed by the statement, "Most religions are alike, aren't they?"

Be careful with variations until you understand why the religion question works so well. The religion question is effective because it allows us to establish that most religions are alike, which gives us common ground. It is also effective because it allows us to immediately deal with the bottom line, the sin issue. Instead of dealing with symptoms of the problem (lack of joy, peace, prosperity, etc.) the Any-3 bridge gets efficiently, yet relationally, to the core issue.

THREE COMMON RESPONSES

When we bridge to a God conversation, people generally respond in one of three ways. In each instance, we turn the conversation back to the basic premise, "Almost all religions are alike, aren't they?"

Response #1:
"I am a Muslim, but I believe all religions are good."
Any-3 Reply: Yes, most religions are alike, aren't they? We are all trying to please God, and we are trying to get our sins forgiven. We are all sinners, aren't we?

Response #2:
"I am a Muslim (then silence)."

Any-3 Reply: Most religions are alike, aren't they? We are all trying to please God, and we are trying to get our sins forgiven. We are all sinners, aren't we?

Response #3:
"I am a Muslim, how about you?"

Any-3 Reply: I was raised in a religious home.[13] I used to try hard to be a good person, so I could please God. However, though I tried to be good, I was never quite good enough. God is in heaven and is holy, but we on the earth are unholy. Through our religion, we try to please God with our good works, but it is never enough. We climb, then fall. Climb, then fall. It's frustrating, isn't it? Most religions are alike, aren't they? We are all trying to please God, to get our sins forgiven.

If you find yourself in response #3, you can also use the "Human Effort Cannot Replace Sins" illustration found in Appendix B.

---

[13] If you were not raised in a religious home, you can still say, "I used to try to please God, but always seemed to fail, and this left me frustrated." Then continue with the standard response, "Most religions are alike...."

6
Telling the Gospel Story

MANY MUSLIM EVANGELISTS have learned that the Old Testament sacrifice stories are a very effective way to proclaim the gospel to Muslims. Early on when the gospel began spreading in our context, we were telling brief versions of five sacrifice stories, concluding with Jesus Christ as the Lamb of God, who takes away the sins of the world. With time, we found it more efficient and effective to begin by sharing the Adam and Eve story, along with the gospel story during the first meeting. We call this story *The First and Last Sacrifice Story.*[14] When we *find* persons who are open to the gospel, we use the other sacrifice stories as material for follow-up.[15]

---

[14] Notice that the story begins by introducing Jesus and then shifts to the Adam and Eve story, before resuming the final part of the Jesus story. We've found that beginning with Jesus allows us to quickly share the gospel if time limitations prevent us from telling the entire *First and Last Sacrifice Story.* Even so, starting with Adam and Eve and then telling the Jesus story is equally effective if time is not an issue.

[15] The shortened versions of the stories we use to follow up open persons are in Appendix A.

THE FIRST AND LAST SACRIFICE STORY

Part One: Jesus

Jesus, the Word of God,[16] was in Heaven with God from the beginning. He was born into this world through the Virgin Mary. Both the Bible and the Qur'an teach this. Jesus never sinned, even though He was tempted in every way imaginable. Jesus overcame the desires of His flesh. He never married; never killed anyone; never gathered riches for Himself.[17] Jesus once fasted 40 days and 40 nights while being tempted by the devil, yet he never sinned.

Jesus performed great miracles. He cast out demons; healed the sick and blind; Jesus even raised the dead.

It is interesting that, though Jesus was not yet old, He began prophesying about His death. To his followers He said, "I must die, but I will rise again." Do you know why Jesus said, "I must die?"[18]

---

[16] Muslims will recognize references to Jesus as the Word of God, His virgin birth and miracles from the Qur'an, *surah al-Imran* 3:42-55. This "Jesus" section parallels much of Kevin Greeson's *The Camel, How Muslims Are Coming to Faith in Christ!* (Richmond: WIGTake Resources, 2007) without actually quoting from the Qur'an. The miracle of casting out demons isn't mentioned in the Qur'an.

[17] This reference to the holy conduct of Jesus puts Him into sharp contrast with Islam's founding prophet.

[18] Although many Muslims believe that Jesus did not die, we speak the truth about His death in *The First and Last Sacrifice Story*. Out of respect, they usually let us finish the story. If they raise an objection at this point we try to delay answering until after the gospel presentation. When the question must be answered, we often refer to Old Testament prophecies concerning Jesus' death. We also mention Qur'anic references, such as 3:55 and 19:33. The first reference clearly states that Jesus died, and surah Miriam 19:33-34 states the Muslim position that Jesus prophesied his death and resurrection: *"And peace is on me the day I was born and the day I will die and the day I am raised alive. That is Jesus, the son of Mary - the word of truth about which they are in dispute."*

Part Two: Why did Jesus have to die?
The Adam and Eve Story

The answer is found in the *Taurat* (what Muslims call the five books of Moses). The *Taurat* tells us about the first persons God created, Adam and Eve. God put them in a perfect paradise, called the Garden of Eden. They were given great freedom to eat fruit from any tree in the garden except for the fruit of the tree of the knowledge of good and evil. God warned them that if they ate of that fruit they would die.

A Covering for Sin
One day, Satan visited Eve in the form of a serpent and tempted her to eat the fruit that God had forbidden. She ate the fruit, and gave it to Adam, who also ate it. Immediately, they were afraid, so they hid from God. But because God knows everything, he found them and punished Adam and Eve for their disobedience

God's Punishment
As punishment for their disobedience, God cast Adam and Eve out of the garden paradise, and eventually they did die. God's desire had been for them to live forever, but because of their sins, they lost paradise and died.

It is interesting that the *Taurat* says Adam and Eve committed just one sin and it resulted in their judgment and death. Adam and Eve seemed like good people, probably better than us. Perhaps they had already done hundreds of good works. They hadn't killed anyone, committed adultery, or stolen anything. But they disobeyed *just once* and it resulted in death. Sometimes we think that if our good deeds outweigh our bad deeds that our sins will be forgiven, but that is not what the Bible says.

Promised Savior and New Clothes
Yet God still loved Adam and Eve. So He made a way for their sins to be forgiven. After pronouncing His judgment on Adam and Eve, God also judged the serpent (Satan) who had deceived them. God promised that from the woman's descendent a Savior would come who would crush Satan's head, although

Satan would also injure Him. Over the centuries that followed, many prophets of God foretold the coming of a Savior who would take away the sins of the world.

Then God did something very interesting. He changed Adam and Eve's clothes. God replaced the clothes made of leaves that Adam and Eve had made with new clothes made from animal skins. Of course, to make these clothes, an animal had to die. The death of an innocent animal was the price that God paid to cover the sins of Adam and Eve. Because He loved Adam and Eve, God himself offered the first sacrifice for the forgiveness of their sins. The Bible teaches us that apart from the shedding of blood, there is no forgiveness of sins (Hebrews 9:22). Since that first sacrifice, all of our forefathers have offered sacrifices to have their sins forgiven: Adam and Eve, Cain and Abel, Noah, Abraham, Moses, David, and others.

Part Three: "That is why Jesus had to die!"

And then Jesus came, born of a virgin, the descendent of a woman. Jesus lived a sinless life, and performed great miracles. At the beginning of Jesus' ministry, a prophet named John looked to Jesus and said, "Look, the Lamb of God, who takes away the sins of the world."

That is interesting, isn't it? Jesus was called "the Lamb of God." Why? Because a lamb is an animal used for sacrifice. Do you remember my question: "Do you know why Jesus said, 'I must die?'" That is why Jesus said, "I must die."

Jesus came to be God's sacrifice to pay for our sins. This is why He surrendered Himself to the Jewish leaders and Roman soldiers to be crucified. He was God's sacrifice for your sins and mine.

As He was dying, Jesus cried out, "It is finished," meaning that our sin debt had now been paid for. Then Jesus bowed His head and died. But on the third day, Jesus rose from the dead, just as He had promised. For the next 40 days, Jesus appeared to more than 500 of His followers, and then was taken up into heaven. We know that one day, Jesus will return to earth as judge over all mankind.

Conclusion: *"That is why I know my sins are forgiven."*
The Bible tells us that if we surrender our life to Jesus as Lord
and believe that He has paid for our sins through his sacrifice
and that God has raised Him from the dead, our sins will be
forgiven. ***And that is why I know my sins are forgiven.***

ANY-3 STORY FEATURES

That is Interesting

Notice that in *The First and Last Sacrifice Story* I periodically use
the phrase "That is interesting." In Any-3, this phrase calls the
hearer's attention to important points that we don't want him
to miss.[19]

The first "interesting" part of this story is that Jesus prophesied
his own death. Next, it is interesting that Adam and Eve were
given the death penalty even though they only committed
one sin. It is also interesting that God changed their clothes,
because this action by God introduces the theme of sacrifice
in Scripture. Finally, it is most interesting that Jesus was called
"The Lamb of God."

Decision Questions: Two Questions help us get to a decision.
First, after sharing *The First and Last Sacrifice Story* ask, "That
makes sense, doesn't it?" Though we cannot pay off our own sin
debt, God has made a way for our sins to be forgiven through
Jesus' sacrificial death and resurrection. Then ask him, "Do you
believe what I have told you: that Jesus died for our sins and
was raised again?"

---

[19] Feel free to use your own tag phrase for "That is interesting." The important
points to emphasize in this story are:1) Sin brought judgment; 2) The effects of sin
were shame, fear, and judgment; 3) Good works can't cancel sins; 4) God's provision
of clothing made from a sacrificed animal foreshadowed His future provision of a
sacrificial Savior.

7
Any-3 Insights

AS WE EXAMINED Jesus' pattern of evangelism with the woman at the well, we could see the five-step pathway that He took. As we look more closely, we gain insights into the character of Jesus' witness. Jesus always witnessed well. As we follow His example, we will do well to emulate these same characteristics.

Intentional

As we pointed out, Jesus *had* to go to Samaria in order to witness to the Samaritan woman. Even though it seemed spontaneous, it was, in fact, intentional. The witness who understands the gospel and is willing and prepared to share it will have opportunities to do so. God will connect such a witness with people who need to hear the gospel, many of whom He has already prepared to receive it.

Christians who *plan* to share the gospel do so much more often than those who passively "wait for the Spirit to lead them." God's word has already commanded us to share the gospel, so the Spirit is already leading us to do so. If we are unfaithful in sharing the gospel, we do not have the Spirit to blame. Prepare to share the gospel. And then make a plan to spend time where lost people are with the intention of sharing the gospel with them.

More than six years ago, a mission volunteer used Any-3 to lead a middle-aged Muslim man named Rauf to Christ. Rauf went on to plant and develop an impressive house church network. Soon after professing faith, Rauf used the same Any-3 process that had reached him to lead a woman in his community named Aisha to faith. Rauf and Aisha were later married. Since that time, Aisha has led more than a hundred Muslim women to Christ through multiplying fellowships of believers.

During Any-3 workshops we train participants to share the gospel, and then send them out to do so. They know that after they go out to share, we will meet again in an accountability session to see how the experience went. Most participants share the gospel at least once immediately following the training. The others generally do so soon after the first accountability session. Many people hear the gospel through Any-3 workshops because we prepare for it. God delights to save people, and shares His delight with those who witness. God honors our obedience more than our spontaneity.

Informal

While prayer walking, a missionary engaged in a casual conversation with a Muslim man named Rizal. Rizal mentioned that his father-in-law would soon be going to Mecca. When the missionary asked Rizal why his father-in-law was planning to go to Mecca, Rizal responded, "To get his sins forgiven." This led to a natural conversation about why good works can't forgive sins. Later that morning, Rizal surrendered himself to Christ as Lord and Savior.

Most of Jesus' witnessing experiences occurred in the course of everyday life. Rather than waiting for a formal religious setting, Jesus witnessed informally. In the case of the Samaritan woman, Jesus witnessed beside a well, not at the synagogue.

Most witnessing opportunities occur in everyday life for modern disciples as well, not in religious settings. In fact, everyday situations usually present great witnessing opportunities. The gospel seems more relevant when presented in the context of daily life. Such witnessing encounters do not feel staged, and the person does not feel set up or manipulated. When we are always prepared to share our faith, Satan has less opportunity to prevent the lost person from receiving the message.

Using Any-3, we witness everywhere and enjoy doing it. The best place to witness is wherever you meet people. Even so, when planning to do Any-3, places where people aren't pressed for time or don't have a competing agenda generally produces the best opportunities to share the gospel.

While prayerfully looking for opportunities to share your faith, enjoy the Any-3 experience. Drink a soft drink or have some tea, hang out and share the gospel with somebody. You might just make a new family member in the process.

The gospel is terrific news, so share it joyfully. Any tension in the witnessing conversation should happen because of the Holy Spirit's conviction not because of the reluctance or nervousness of the witness. It is fun to be the bearer of good news.

Any-3 takes place in an informal, natural way. By the way, if anyone, anywhere in the world invites you to sit down and talk, what they are actually saying is, "Share the gospel with me."

Interactive

When Jesus shared the gospel with the woman at the well, he could have pointed his finger and preached at her, but He didn't. Jesus never acted condescending or condemning. Instead, he was interactive and engaging.

According to the episode in John's Gospel, Jesus spoke seven times and the Samaritan woman spoke six times in their conversation (John 4:7-26). Jesus' interactive style was His pattern throughout the witnessing encounter.

The early tone of Jesus' conversation with the woman was relaxed. The tone changed later. However, tension did not occur in the transition to spiritual matters. Rather the tone changed when the conversation became personal. Tension only entered the conversation when conviction entered as Jesus identified the woman's personal sin and began to call for a response.

One Any-3 trainer told me, "The folks that I trained in one group were reluctant to witness. They told me that they had tried a more confrontational approach to evangelism, and were shell-shocked as a result. After learning Any-3, though, they have once again become bold witnesses. They said that they found the interactive yet intentional style of Any-3 to be more natural for them."

One of the greatest challenges for the witness is to witness with the same relaxed tone of voice and mannerisms as when talking about non-spiritual things. Even in the transition to spiritual matters, the conversation should maintain a very informal, relaxed tone.

On the other hand, we must remember, that the gospel of Jesus Christ can also produce in the hearer an intense inner battle. At this point, the Holy Spirit is drawing the person to a commitment. Tension of this kind is not a negative, but rather a vital part of the process of conversion. The key is for the witness himself not to introduce tension through personal nervousness, needless arguments or a preachy lecture. Let the Holy Spirit do the work of conviction, while the witness helps to guide the person to the truth.

If legitimate questions do arise, offer to answer them later, but do not be argumentative. People are rarely won to Christ through arguments no matter how persuasive they may be. Instead, focus on giving a simple, loving presentation of the gospel.

Initiative

Once a very conservative Muslim, Jamila came to faith through her husband's witness. Since that time, using Any-3, Jamila has reached hundreds of Muslim women with the gospel. Jamila's efforts have led to the formation of more than 100 groups of various generations, many of which have become house churches. Jamila's fruitfulness isn't by accident. She takes the initiative to drive her relationships and conversations toward a gospel presentation and a decision for Christ.

When Jesus initiated the conversation with the woman at the well, He also took the initiative to guide the conversation to its intended goal. Without being preachy or condescending Jesus still assumed the role of teacher as the conversation progressed. He asked pointed questions aimed at leading the woman to the ultimate goal of a decision for Christ.

Witnesses today should emulate Jesus' approach. In building rapport we meet on a person-to-person level. As the conversation turns toward the gospel, we must take the initiative and lead.

We call this *guiding the conversation*. People who use Any-3 most effectively find the appropriate balance between interaction and initiative. Too much interaction places the conversation in the lost person's hands. The lost will rarely steer the conversation toward their need for salvation. It's up to the witness to make this happen.

Jesus guided the conversation at the well. Often, the woman raised issues that were not directed toward Jesus' plan, so he gently redirected the conversation. Jesus only followed after issues that were heading toward the gospel. Look again at the passage; see how Jesus guided the conversation. Notice that Jesus might naturally have said something else in response to her statements, but He chose to lead instead of just going along for the ride.

Let's return to John 4:7-26 to see how Jesus did this. When we first meet the woman, she was minding her own business, until Jesus asked her for a drink (v. 7). Instead of discussing cultural and religious differences, He brought up the topic of Living Water (v. 10). Instead of debating whether He was greater than Jacob, Jesus stayed with the topic of Living Water (vv. 12-14). The Savior's most interesting initiative was when the woman asked for the living water (v. 15). Instead of granting her request, He told her to call her husband to come there. Further, Jesus taught about worshipping in spirit and in truth, rather than about the woman's preferred topic, the place of worship. Finally, Jesus let the woman decide where the conversation would go, because it was where He wanted to take it. "I who am speaking to you," he said, "am He" (v. 26).

Introducing the Messiah

As Jesus' witnessing conversation progressed, the Samaritan woman became increasingly aware of who Jesus was. Her understanding increased from Jesus being a Jewish man (v. 9), to perhaps being greater than Jacob (v. 12), to being a prophet (v. 19), to being the Messiah (vv. 25-26). Jesus' goal is to help all people understand that He is the promised Savior. Likewise, this is the goal of every witnessing conversation.

Jesus was witnessing to the Samaritan woman before his sacrificial death and resurrection had occurred. Even so, He introduced Himself as the Messiah. Many Jews in those days awaited a Messianic deliverer, one who would restore Israel's glory. The Samaritan woman's understanding would have been somewhat different. She expected the Messiah to be a source of truth, as well as a deliverer.

What does it mean for us to share the Messiah with others today? Jesus gave a clear answer to his disciples after His resurrection in Luke 24:44, 46-48.

> *Now He said to them, 'These are my words which I spoke to you while I was still with you, that all things which are written about Me in the Law of Moses and the Prophets and the Psalms must be fulfilled.' Then He said to them, 'Thus it is written, that the Christ would suffer and rise again from the dead the third day, and that repentance for forgiveness of sins would be proclaimed in His name to all the nations, beginning from Jerusalem. You are witnesses of these things.'*

Jesus commissioned his witnesses to proclaim that the Christ must suffer for our sins, die and rise again. Those who repent and believe this gospel have forgiveness of sins. This is the gospel that Jesus proclaimed after His resurrection. This is also the message preached by Paul and the apostles (1 Corinthians 15:1-4). The apostle Peter repeated the same message in 1 Peter 3:18. This is the same gospel that we are to share today.

Ali has become a very effective Muslim evangelist who shares the gospel immediately with everyone he meets. Some years ago, before coming to faith in Christ, Ali took a job in a city that was far away from his home. While he was in that city, Ali met several times with a missionary who lived there. Each time they met, the missionary shared some biblical truths with Ali. After several meetings, though, the relationship ended. Ali looks back now on that relationship and with consternation in his voice says, "That missionary never shared the gospel with me." Sharing biblical truths is good, but if we fail to introduce the Messiah, we have missed the heart of the gospel.

Personal testimonies about peace and love, comments about Jesus' wisdom and power, and discussions from the holy books of other religions may at times be beneficial, but remember, only the gospel has the power to save. For this reason, the gospel should be the primary message the witness shares. Be a bearer of the best news, the news that sin has been paid for!

Capture What You've Learned

Any-3 Insights

1. *Intentional*
2. *Informal*
3. *Interactive*
4. *Initiative*
5. *Introducing the Messiah*

Any-3 Communication Tips

Along with the five Any-3 insights, here are a few practical communication tips that will help you become a more effective witness for Christ.

Speak his language.

Adjustments in communication are the responsibility of the speaker, not the listener. So, plan to adjust the way you communicate in order to be heard with as little misunderstanding as possible.

A translator can help to bridge language barriers for expat mission volunteers. The translator should be trained to avoid terminology that might be misunderstood by the hearer. The goal is to explain who Jesus is according to the Scripture while using religious terms that are already familiar to the recipient. This way, the recipient will actually hear the gospel, rather than closing the conversation before the gospel is presented.

Even though the approach to witnessing may vary depending on who is being evangelized, do not let the complexity of witnessing to different kinds of people inhibit you from sharing with them. It is far more important that a lost person hear and understand the gospel, than it is for you to understand all the things that make this person's religion or culture unique.

Listen to what he believes

Asking personal questions builds rapport that is necessary for witnessing well. Early in a witnessing conversation, it is important to let the other person do most of the talking, because later you will guide the conversation. When you ask a lot of questions to get the other person engaged in the conversation, the person witnessed to will more likely listen politely later as the witness shares the gospel with him.

Being "a little bit dumb" is actually better than being "too smart." Appearing to know too much about the person's religion and culture, often makes the person being witnessed to uncomfortable. This may cause him to put up his guard. The best way to learn about a person is to ask him about himself and what he believes. Asking questions not only teaches you what the person believes and what makes him unique, it allows you to tailor your witness to that particular individual.

Show respect

When you witness often, you may become task oriented rather than people oriented. Discipline yourself to enjoy each witnessing experience as a person who is sharing wonderful news with another person.

Keep in mind that the person you're witnessing to is not an evangelism target; he's a person. In fact, he's a lost person. Remember that you, too, were once lost, so you should understand this situation. Whether rich or poor, good or bad is irrelevant; he's in the same condition as all of mankind -- a sinner in need of the Savior.

8
Be-e Stings
That Poison Effectiveness

I N JOHN 4:35, Jesus said, "Lift up your eyes, look on the fields, that they are white for harvest." This has never been more true than today. As we enter into these harvest fields, though, we find a number of *be-es* that Satan uses to *sting* our ministry and prevent a productive harvest.

A fruitful harvest requires deliberate planning and effort. Successful harvesters have learned to identify and overcome the *be-e stings* that Satan sends their way and bring in the crop to harvest. Let me share with you some of the *be-e stings* that we identified and had to overcome to get to a fruitful harvest.

Be-e Really Careful!

When missionaries prepare to enter countries that are hostile to the gospel they sometimes hear: "Your goal is to live among the people for a long time, so do not be too aggressive in sharing the gospel or you may be deported. Worse yet, you might get us all kicked out!"

We become afraid of what *might* happen if we share the gospel boldly. Paralyzed with uncertainty, we let witnessing opportunities pass us by. Though persecution is real, it should never preclude obedience to the Great Commission. Most "what ifs" are actually excuses provided by the enemy aimed at stifling Christian witness.

The temptation to be overly cautious is not a new one. In Acts 4:29-30, after his imprisonment, Peter prayed, "Now, Lord, consider their threats and enable your servants to speak your word with great boldness." Peter and the early church identified persecution as providential in origin, and prayed for greater boldness in sharing the good news!

The turning point for our own ministry came when we decided to share the gospel with anyone, anywhere, anytime. We put the results and consequences in God's hands and obeyed. As a result, the new believers caught this same attitude, and shared the gospel unbound by chains of fear.

Be-e Sting: Bad things may happen, so I must be really careful about witnessing.

Be-e Sting Antidote: Realistically evaluate security concerns, count the cost, and then share the gospel more freely. God is sovereign over all things. If bad things happen, they will likely facilitate kingdom growth in the end.

Be-e Really Smart!

Perhaps you have heard the warning: "You cannot share the gospel over here the way you did in America." This warning implies that Christian workers must master their host culture and religion before they can share the gospel. *Really smart evangelism* expects every effective evangelist to be an expert and an entrepreneurial witness.

Classes on Christian missions, sometimes highlight the silly mistakes that Christian workers have made in their ministries. Nobody wants to be the example of using bone-headed techniques that later become the case study for what not to do as a Christian worker. Fear of mistakes, can easily inhibit our evangelistic zeal.

Ironically, we have found that when it comes to evangelism, being a little bit dumb may be better than being too smart.

Revealing expertise in the local culture can provoke defensiveness from the Muslims with whom you are sharing. Using an Any-3 approach, and asking questions, even when you already know the answer, lays a foundation of mutual respect.

After all, what is the best way to learn about a new culture than spending time with the people? Ask local persons what they believe; this is the way Any-3 begins. As you listen and learn, you will become more effective in sharing the gospel.

Ali is a very gifted evangelist who used to use many different Quranic verses as a bridge, often taking as many as three visits just to get to the gospel. These days, Ali is relying on the power of the gospel to find open persons. Ali says, "I used to use the Quran as a bridge, but with Any-3 I no longer have to guess who is going to be open to the gospel." Ali regularly leads conservative Muslims to faith, whom he immediately baptizes. Streams from Ali's work are now multigenerational, with each generation using Any-3 as their default evangelism method.

Be-e **Sting:** I must deeply understand my people group's culture and religion, before I share the gospel with them.

Be-e **Sting Antidote:** The gospel is relevant in every context. So, learn all you can about your community, and while you do, share the gospel frequently. The interactive nature of Any-3 is a great way to learn more about the target culture and religious beliefs while you witness.

Be-e a Friend Maker!

How long does it take to develop a friendship and earn a hearing? My friend Bill approached me recently with this dilemma; "I have known my Muslim friend for six months now. When should I share the gospel with him?"

The friendship *be-e sting* assumes, "They must like me, before they will like my Jesus." We think that by befriending people first, they will know that we genuinely care about them and are not just trying to impose our religion on them.

Contrast this with my colleague Kevin who recently said, "As far as I know, all of my friends have now heard the gospel."

Kevin had previously been less effective as he spent a long time developing friendships first, but now he shares the gospel immediately.

Friendship evangelism raises more questions than it answers. "Will my witness put a strain on the relationship I have worked so hard to build? Will my friend wonder why I waited so long to share with him? Will my friend be open to the gospel once I do share with him?"

Being a friend is great, but a lost person shouldn't have to become my personal friend to hear about Jesus from me. I might be introverted or socially awkward. We may have differing personalities or interests. They may not have time to befriend me. They may feel more comfortable relating deeply with someone of their own culture. I may intimidate them. Even so, everyone deserves to hear the gospel. After all, I may never see them again.

Friendship evangelism also fails on a practical level. Building friendships takes lots of time and energy. How long would it take to reach the world through friendship evangelism, if it takes so long to get to the gospel? The truth is, we can only maintain a limited number of close friendships.

If we share the gospel immediately, we can be certain that those who become our friends will know the gospel and know our commitment to it. Otherwise, we might spend years developing a friendship before sharing the gospel, only to discover that our friend is not interested.

We are finding that when we share the gospel immediately with lost persons, they are more often coming to faith than when we delay or only share with them step by step over a period of time. God is moving them from pre-evangelism to sincere faith, often during the first meeting. This may seem illogical, but it reveals the work of the Holy Spirit in convicting and regenerating the lost.

Be-e Sting: Tie friendship to sharing the gospel. Delay sharing the gospel until a solid friendship has been developed.

Be-e **Sting Antidote:** Be friendly, and share the gospel early in every relationship. The best friends are those who have heard the gospel and still want to be around us. If someone distances himself or herself from us because of the gospel, they would not likely have made a very good friend anyway. On the other hand, if someone hears the gospel from us and still wants to be our friend, it is a good sign that he or she might be open to the gospel and become a good friend as well.

Be-e A Quiet Example!

Another stinger is confusing good Christian behavior with communicating the gospel. Good Christians show the love of Christ by their actions. But if we think that, "People will see my good actions and ask about why my life is different," we are probably deceiving ourselves. Even though it sounds good, how often do the lost approach a Christian asking him to share the gospel with them? It is rare. This is the problem with "being a really quite example:" it places the responsibility for a witness on the lost rather than on us.

Though people should see Christ-like characteristics in us, when they examine us more closely, they will doubtless see our glaring flaws as well. Even those closest to Jesus, the original disciples, who could make the best claim to Christlikeness, obediently shared the gospel. Their lifestyle supported but did not replace the proclamation of the gospel.

The truth is that people only get saved when they hear the gospel (Romans 10:14-17). Yes, they could read the gospel for themselves and be saved, but they will not read it in our lives unless, perhaps, it has been written on our clothing. Salvation requires a presentation of the gospel. Your life, no matter how good, is no substitute for a gospel presentation.

Be-e **Sting:** Living a godly life is as good as sharing the gospel.

Be-e **Sting Antidote:** Live a godly life while joyfully sharing the gospel with anyone, anywhere, and anytime.

Be-e Really Generous!

Christians are generous people. Freely we have received and so we freely give. However, when we link sharing the gospel with meeting the physical needs of the lost we run the risk of confusing the two. Physical needs are here today, and gone tomorrow. Eternal salvation is forever. While it is perfectly appropriate to integrate human needs ministries with gospel witness, we must never delay sharing the gospel until physical needs are met.

Even in Jesus' day this challenge existed. After Jesus fed the 5,000, there were some who came to follow Him for the wrong reasons. Jesus said, "Truly, truly I say to you, you seek Me, not because you saw signs, but because you ate of the loaves and were filled" (John 6:26-27a). The purpose of Jesus' miracle, and of human needs ministries today is to point people to Jesus as the Christ, the Son of God (John 20:31).

Though persons can be reached through social ministries, we often find that recipients of aid confuse genuine interest in Christ with a desire for aid and services. This becomes evident when they lose their spiritual interest as soon as the monetary kindness has ceased.

One of our colleagues named Luke had mastered the local language and used community development during the majority of his first term as a platform to share the gospel. Despite these advantages, Luke saw very little obvious evangelistic fruit, although he desperately desired it. After receiving a crash course in Any-3, Luke began proclaiming the gospel more quickly and intentionally drawing the net. Within a half year, dozens of people had professed faith, and seven new groups were formed.

We are finding the best disciples come from those who respond to the gospel because they are hungry for righteousness. They have come to submit to Christ as Lord. Using Any-3, we are finding hundreds of people who are "selling all" to follow Christ without any hope of payment from us. God becomes their treasure, and they minister to one another's personal needs as the body of Christ.

Be-e **Sting:** Give people employment or benefits and meet their physical needs so they will be open to a gospel witness.

Be-e **Sting Antidote:** Share the gospel without condition while lovingly yet discreetly helping those in need. As the apostle Paul said, "while we have opportunity, let us do good to all men, and especially to those who are of the household of the faith" (Galatians 6:10).

Be-e Really Incarnational!

In an incarnational approach, a missionary seeks to become a meaningful part of the community by adopting the local culture and language. This is well and good, but can also become an endless pursuit of acceptance, as a prerequisite to gospel witness.

Every Christian should strive to live a Christ-like life in their community as an example of holiness before the people they hope to reach. After all, wasn't Jesus just an incarnational missionary? Well, yes and no. Jesus *did* live his life incarnationally, but that is *not* how he accomplished his mission!

If Jesus' primary goal was to incarnationally reach His own community, He failed. Jesus lived for some 30 years as a perfect man in Galilee before He began His public ministry. His own incarnational lifestyle was filled with perfect wisdom and modeled a perfect life. And yet, until after the resurrection, almost all of the people in Jesus' community rejected Him.

Jesus' own relatives concluded that He had lost His mind; His neighbors esteemed Him no higher than a carpenter's son or an ordinary member of the community, prompting Jesus to conclude, "A prophet is not without honor except in his own home town and among his kinsmen" (Mark 3:21, 6:4).

Jesus lived incarnationally, but He accomplished His mission relationally and exponentially. Jesus went beyond his community to reach disciples and accomplish His mission.

In John chapter one, we see how Jesus accomplished this mission. Jesus Himself called His earliest disciples, Andrew and John. Afterwards, Andrew introduced his brother Peter to

Jesus. Jesus then led Philip to faith, and Philip led his friend Nathanael. These occurrences show us that while Jesus reached the first generation of converts, these converts then reached their own network of friends and family, what the Bible calls their *oikos*[20] (John 1:35-51).

Where incarnational missions can miss the mark is when a missionary satisfies himself with first-generation evangelism. Jesus went further, training first-generation converts to reach their *oikos*. The first generation must do second-generation evangelism and so forth until multiplying generations are reached.

The basic flaw of applying the principle of incarnational evangelism to cross-cultural workers is that the cross-cultural worker has left his own *oikos* to work in a different cultural community, one in which he has no family or *oikos*. God's solution for this is to raise up persons of peace -- persons prepared by the Holy Spirit to receive the gospel -- who will come to faith from the foreign worker's witness and then take the gospel to their own, much larger, *oikos*.

Be-e Sting: The incarnational life becomes an end in itself. Becoming *like* one's adopted community becomes primary, while sharing the gospel becomes secondary.

Be-e Sting Antidote: Witness broadly both inside and outside your community and platform in order to find persons of peace. When you find these persons of peace, train them to reach their own *oikos* and communities with the gospel.

Be-e Really Busy!

Being busy is certainly better in almost every case than being lazy. It is true that lazy people aren't likely to lead many people to faith, but neither are extremely busy people. That is, unless they intentionally set aside time to share the gospel.

---

[20] *Oikos* is the Greek word for extended household. It referred to one's immediate family, extended family immediate friends and associates within one's sphere of influence.

The problem with busyness is that doing good things can take away time and energy from doing the best things. Because witnessing doesn't come naturally for most people, we must prioritize and schedule times to be where people are in order to share the gospel with them. Some of the most likely people to lead others to faith have filled their schedules with good, but not best practices.

For many people busyness becomes a 'way out' of doing evangelism. We tend to make time for the things we enjoy and procrastinate from doing those we dread. Therefore, we often fill our schedules with actions related to our strengths and perceived giftedness, while neglecting what is perhaps Christ's most urgent command for all believers, "You shall be my witnesses" (Acts 1:8b).

It's astounding to think about how many people don't share the gospel because they "don't have time." Many well-meaning Christians decide to share the gospel more often, but fail because they haven't quit doing something important in order to start sharing the gospel more intentionally. What will you stop doing in order to intentionally share the gospel more often? Good things happen in God's kingdom when we replace good things with the 'main thing'.

Be-e **Sting:** Doing good things crowds out doing the 'main thing' (evangelism).

Be-e **Sting Antidote:** Replace some less important activity by setting aside time to practice Any-3 and training others to do so.

BURNING DOWN THE BEE HIVE

In nature, once a bee stings a person, the bee dies. In missions, these *be-e stings* can go on for years. The solution is to burn down the hive! The following tips will help you get over your bee stings and move on.

The Hearing Has Been Earned

Each of the preceding *be-e stings* presupposes that Christians must earn a hearing for the gospel. In fact, Christ has already earned that right. When Christ paid for our sins, He also earned the right for us to share the gospel. Christ has given us the authority to "proclaim the gospel to every creature" (Mark 16:15).

The gospel saves, not because of perfect messengers, but because of the worthy Lord who accomplished it.

Why They're Professing Faith

Recently, in the Asian country where I serve, we surveyed Muslim-background believers, asking them, "What did God use to bring you to faith in Christ?" We expected to hear a range of reasons for this radical life change.

The most common answer was that -- for the first time -- someone had told them the gospel message that Jesus died as a sacrifice for the forgiveness of their sins. Quite simply, these Muslims gave their lives to Christ because they heard the gospel and were invited to surrender themselves to Him.

People come to faith because they *hear* the gospel and are invited to respond to it. There is no substitute for direct mouth-to-ear evangelism.

The Gospel Is the Filter

The only way to know who is open to the gospel is to share it with them, and see who responds. Religious affiliation, clothing, body language, and intuition are very poor substitutes. After you share the gospel, you will know within minutes, rather than days or months, who is open and responsive.

After we share the gospel using the *First and Last Sacrifice Story* (see Chapter Six), we ask two questions to draw the net. The second question, "Do you believe it?" is the filter question. While their facial expressions and body language may give some hint of their interest or lack thereof, you will never really know if they believe the gospel until you ask them.

Two Questions to Gauge Openness

1. This story makes sense, doesn't it? We cannot pay off our own sins, but God arranged forgiveness of sins through Christ's sacrifice.

2. Do you believe it?

Do Evangelism, Not Pre-Evangelism

In our country, we try to share the gospel with a Muslim in our first meeting with them. Doing so, we have found them to be much more likely to say yes to Jesus, than when we wait to share the gospel until much later in the relationship.

Before coming to faith in Christ, Jamaal had been a jihadi militant. A recently baptized believer set aside his fears to approach Jamaal with the gospel, and Jamaal surrendered himself to Christ. Together, these two men, along with another friend formed a team that within six months led 200 people to faith and started 12 new house churches.

Jesus and His apostles routinely did evangelism in their first meeting with someone, and so can we. The first three steps of Any-3 set the stage for the gospel, but within 10-15 minutes after saying "Hello," you can be sharing the gospel.

9

Any-3 Bridges to Success - Motivations

JESUS' EARLY DISCIPLES had a lot in common with His disciples today -- we both need a motivation to witness, and an example to follow. This is why Jesus invited His disciples into His witnessing experience with the woman at the well (John 4:1-45). This also explains why the Holy Spirit had John record the lesson for Jesus' disciples today. With the woman at the well, Jesus modeled five motivations that would inspire His disciples to witness to anyone, anywhere, at any time. He used the analogy of a harvest to explain.

Passion for the Harvest

While Jesus was preparing to witness to a lost woman, His disciples went into the city to buy food (John 4:8). While they were gone, they missed an opportunity to participate in Jesus' witnessing encounter.

When they returned from their meal the disciples found Jesus violating two deeply ingrained Jewish traditions: 1) Jews do not fellowship with Samaritans, and 2) Men do not talk to women in public. Unsure how to respond, they offered Jesus something to eat.

But Jesus had already "eaten." It appears that the Savior always "packed His lunch" and had just finished it. "My food is to do

the will of Him who sent Me and to accomplish His work"
(John 4:34). Jesus would rather witness than eat! That modeled
for the disciples His passion for the harvest. In the same way
that you or I *have to* eat ice cream or our favorite food when it's
sitting in front of us, Jesus *had to* witness. It was His passion.

Passion for the harvest immediately calls to mind an 80-year
old 4th-generation Muslim-background believer named Yahya
who led his friend Musa to Christ. Musa was 83 years old!
Musa immediately became burdened for his family members
who were lost, and rode his rusty old bicycle 21 miles to the
village to share the gospel with them.

Pressure of the Harvest

Jesus impressed on His disciples' minds the urgency of the
harvest. "Do you not say, 'There are yet four months, and then
comes the harvest'? Behold, I say to you, lift up your eyes and
look on the fields, that they are white for harvest" (John 4:35).
If the disciples did not ratchet up the intensity of their witness,
people would perish in the same way that over-ripe wheat
perishes when the harvest is delayed.

Just as it was harvest time for Jesus' disciples, it is now the
time for today's disciples to witness with pressing urgency.
Every day, untold thousands perish, many of whom would be
open to the gospel if only they were to hear it. According to
Jesus, the pressure is on. It is harvest time.

Promise of the Harvest

The promise of the harvest is that sowing leads to reaping. Jesus
demonstrated for His disciples that both sowing and reaping
were the responsibility of every disciple. Jesus said, "*Already*
he who reaps is receiving wages and is gathering fruit for life
eternal; so that he who sows and he who reaps may rejoice
together" (John 4:36).

The goal of the harvest is never just sowing. Only a very foolish
farmer would sow a field that he never intended to reap. Even
worse would be to just remove stones from the field, so that some

future Christians could sow or reap. Sowing seed is hard, hot, tiring work, but the promise of a harvest makes it worthwhile.

In every witnessing encounter, sow and reap expectantly. Jesus taught His disciples that a harvest can mature overnight (Mark 4:26-29). At other times, we may reap the fruit of another's labor (John 4:37).

I like to tell people the story of when four local partners and I shared the gospel with several Muslims in an area where there were no believers or churches. From our perspective, nothing outstanding happened that day. There were no apparent decisions for Christ.

More than a year later, though, two mission volunteers went to the same area and shared the gospel using Any-3. Within half an hour, the Lord had connected them with a man we had shared with two years earlier. As they talked, the man told them, "About a year ago someone shared this good news with me and gave me a small tract. I have read it almost every evening since then." He then prayed to receive Christ.

We celebrated together with overflowing joy. In the days that followed, the man was baptized and reached his family with the gospel, forming the first church in his area.

Produce of the Harvest

Multiplication is built into creation. Every stalk of wheat contains enough seed to produce multiple new plants. Each resulting plant has the same potential for multi-generational reproduction.

People have the same produce potential. Upon hearing the good news about Jesus the Messiah, the woman at the well left her water pot and witnessed to her friends (John 4:29). The Bible says, she called her friends to come and meet Jesus (John 4:28-29). "And from that city many of the Samaritans believed in Him because of the word of the woman who testified" (John 4:39).

It was a worthwhile investment of time for Jesus and his disciples to spend two unplanned days in Samaria in order to equip persons of peace to reach their respective *oikos* (extended family and friends) for Christ.

When my partner Zack and I began daily sowing the gospel among our unreached Muslim people, it was nearly eight months before we saw a harvest. When the harvest came, though, it was full of produce potential. One man that we witnessed to in a public park heard the gospel and believed it. Then he said to us, "I know 50 people who need to hear this message." Indeed, 50 people did hear the gospel very quickly from this man. He has since led hundreds of persons to faith in Christ.

Seeing the produce in the harvest makes the Great Commission attainable. None of us could lead enough people to faith in our lifetime to make a dent in the world's lostness. However, realizing the potential produce of each new believer encourages us to share the gospel and expect God to multiply its produce.

Payment for the Harvest

Nuh's life was headed for a dead-end because of both moral and business failures. Since giving his life to Christ, Nuh has been instrumental in leading his large family and more than 30 others to faith in his conservative Muslim neighborhood. With tears welling up in his eyes, Nuh confessed with deepest appreciation, "Where would my life have been had someone not shared the gospel with me?"

The payment for the harvest is the great joy that we experience as we lead someone to Christ. Jesus said, "Already he who reaps is receiving wages, and is gathering fruit for life eternal; that he who sows and he who reaps may rejoice together"(John 4:36). The one who reaps already receives wages (John 4:36a), and will receive further wages (John 4:36b). Payday is both now and later for the harvester, but the wage is the same now and later.

Nothing satisfies a farmer more than bringing in a successful harvest. There are other motivations for witnessing such as seeing God's glory manifest, and obedience to Christ's Great Commission. Nonetheless, few motivations exceed the sheer joy of seeing people moving from death to life. Let what brings joy to heaven (Luke 15:7), joy in the presence of the angels of God (Luke 14:10), and joy to the Father (Luke 15:32) bring joy to you as well.

Capture What You've Learned
Five Motivations to Become a Harvester

1. *Passion for the Harvest (4:31-34)*
   Jesus would rather evangelize than eat.

2. *Pressure of the Harvest (4:35)*
   The field's readiness determines harvest time.

3. *Promise of the Harvest (4:37-38)*
   Sowing leads to reaping.

4. *Produce of the Harvest (4:28-30)*
   Each new believer can potentially multiply.

5. *Payment for the Harvest (4:36)*
   The farmer's reward is the harvest itself.

10

Any-3 Bridges to Success - The Message

ANY-3 HAS SHOWN you how easy it can be to connect with a lost person, but what about the heart of our message? The most powerful resource we have as Christians is the gospel that we proclaim. Let's take a few minutes to examine the power of the gospel message and make certain that we don't obscure it.

Maximize the Cross's Power

The apostle Paul said, "For Christ did not send me to baptize, but to preach the gospel, not in cleverness of speech, ***so that the cross of Christ would not be made void***" (1 Corinthians 1:17). When the presentation of the gospel is cloaked in human wisdom, more is lost than gained. Using clever introductory bridges to get to the gospel, runs the risk of diminishing the gospel's power. In such cases, the gospel becomes lost among the many truths about Jesus, rather than the one and only truth that saves us. Paul's main objective was to communicate the gospel. *Effective evangelists share the gospel, and they do it early in the relationship.*

The game of golf offers a useful illustration between two differing approaches to evangelism. Some evangelists use introductory bridges to lay a foundation for the gospel. These bridges become the "drivers" aimed at getting the conversation to the green, where a winning putt can be made. After using their favorite introductory driver, these evangelists use other approaches until they sense that they are getting the person close to a decision for Christ. At that point, they pull out the last club in their golf bag, the putter or gospel, and use it to share the message of salvation and press for a decision. The gospel functions as their last club, their putter.

In Any-3, after we connect with a lost person, we pull out the most powerful club in the golf bag, the driver, and use this club to present the gospel. For the Any-3 witness, it is the driver that delivers the gospel, rather than the putter. Other approaches might be used for a follow-up visit, but by then the gospel has already been shared, and used to filter the person's response to the gospel itself. The gospel is your most powerful club, so drive with it.

That is what the first-century church did. They did not play golf, but they did do effective evangelism. One is hard-pressed to find a single New Testament example where the witness delayed the presentation of the gospel past the first visit. They *drove* with the gospel.

Too often, we forget that God still uses simple methods to save people just as He did 2000 years ago. Do we really think we can create witnessing bridges that will enhance the gospel's power? To the contrary, God's saving power is released when we let the gospel rather than the bridge become central.

ANY-3 GOSPEL ASSUMPTIONS

The Gospel is Sacrificial Atonement

The central message of the Bible is God's substitutionary sacrifice for mankind's sins. Beginning in the first book of the Bible, God prophesied the coming of a Savior (Genesis 3:15). This verse was the first of numerous prophecies about a suffering

Savior. The Gospels present Jesus as that suffering Savior, the Lamb of God, who takes away the sins of the world. The New Testament concludes with the second coming of the Lamb of God, whose robe is dipped in blood (Revelation 19:13).

God replaced the makeshift clothes of the first sinners, Adam and Eve, with animal skins (Genesis 3:21). God himself offered the first sacrifice for the forgiveness of sins, since an animal had to die to cover the effects of man's sin. The first human descendants, Cain and Abel, offered sacrifices in worship to God. Of the two sacrifices, it was Abel's animal sacrifice that was acceptable to God. After the flood, Noah offered animal sacrifices in keeping with the faith that had justified him.

Clearly, the Bible reveals the sacrificial system as God's plan of redemption for mankind (Hebrews 9:22). Under the Law of Moses, all righteous people were to offer animal sacrifices to atone for their sins until Christ himself offered the final sacrifice. Suspended on the cross, Jesus cried out, "It is finished!" indicating the fulfillment of God's righteous requirement for sacrifice. Today, it is the job of every witness to proclaim, "Christ has also once suffered for sins, the Just for the unjust at a time appointed by God. He was put to death in the flesh, but made alive by the Spirit" (2 Peter 3:15).

The profound and powerful message of effective evangelism is the simple gospel. Evangelism that confuses this gospel with more complicated methods only weakens the gospel's power.

The Gospel is Good News

While on his way to do Any-3 evangelism in a completely different area, a missions volunteer met a Muslim man named Hussein. Working with his translator, the volunteer was able to share the gospel with Hussein, and Hussein was ripe to respond. Hussein told the volunteer, "This is what I've been waiting to hear!" Soon afterwards, Hussein's family and three others surrendered their lives to Christ, and formed the first church in their village.

Gospel literally means "good news." When the Holy Spirit awakens lost persons to understand the good news, they grasp just how wonderful it is. It is God's gift of salvation.

Jesus commanded his disciples to proclaim the gospel and declared that his disciples would do this throughout the earth (Luke 24:44-48). The heart of the apostles' message was the gospel: that Christ died for our sins, and rose from the dead on the third day (1 Corinthians 15:1-4; 1 Peter 3:18). Those who surrender themselves to Christ as Lord and believe the gospel will be saved (Romans 10:9-10).

The Gospel Is Unique

Most religions teach a system of works as a way of getting to God. Only the Christian faith shows how God himself, not man, took the initiative to redeem sinful people. When a person surrenders to Christ and believes the gospel, his sins are fully forgiven.

In Any-3, the witness begins the conversation by stating that *most* religions are alike. His final objective, though, is to show that the gospel is different.

I also used to take for granted that Christian ministers and missionaries understood the importance of actually communicating that gospel message. Some years ago, though, when teaching an evangelism course I explained to the ministry students that evangelism means conveying the gospel message, and not just talking about Jesus. The light suddenly turned on for one of the students who responded, "You mean that a person must hear the gospel before he can be saved!" Yes, he got it! Since then, this student has become a wonderful witness and led a number of people to Christ.

11

Any-3 Bridges to Success - The Messenger

SUCCESSFUL EVANGELISM IS a gift from God, but it does not drop down from the sky. Effective evangelism does not come naturally; it comes spiritually through learning to abide in Christ, through watching others witness, and through practicing it yourself.

When Jesus said, "Follow Me, and I will make you become fishers of men" (Mark 1:17) He was saying that those who follow Jesus will become evangelists. When we treat evangelism as merely one of the Christian virtues, it rarely produces much fruit. When evangelism becomes our passion as we walk day by day with Christ, it produces much fruit.

Over the past three years, while nurturing a growing church-planting movement, I have immersed myself in Jesus' *Upper Room Discourses* found in John 13-17. In those chapters, Jesus revealed the secret to evangelistic fruitfulness: abiding in Him. Abiding in Christ means being filled with the Holy Spirit, the Spirit of Christ (John 14:16-23).

Spiritual fruitfulness is the overflow of abiding in Christ (John 15:1-8). This passage reminds us that evangelism is more than saying the right words; it is staying connected to the Vine. Some Christians who determine to become witnesses for Christ become frustrated because "the plan didn't work." Effective evangelism is so much more than just implementing a well-devised plan. It grows out of living in an intimate relationship with Jesus Christ, and leading others to believe the gospel and enter into that same kind of relationship.

In addition to challenging His disciples to abide in Him, Jesus gave them a pattern for doing so. Abiding in Christ begins with *absolute surrender* to Christ, a willingness to die (John 12:24; 15:13). Abiding in Christ also requires *humility* (John 13:1-17). We need humility to make the adjustments necessary to obey Christ (John 13:6-10). Humility also keeps us in a proper relationship with one another (John 13:12-17). Dying to ourselves and making lifestyle adjustments in obedience to Christ's word are essential to abiding in Christ and doing His works.

With these prerequisites -- absolute surrender and humility -- we are prepared to abide in Christ through His Walk, His Word, and His Works. These are the keys to experiencing fruitfulness. Christ's used the Upper Room Discourse to prepare His disciples to fulfill the Great Commission. Let's look more closely at humility and surrender, and our three keys to abiding in Christ.

HUMILITY AND SURRENDER

Humility

Among the many profound conversations that occurred in the upper room, none was more significant than those recorded in John 13:1-11. Jesus washed the feet of His disciples, even the feet of Judas who was about to betray Him. Jesus humbled Himself below the lowest of the low, and taught His disciples to do the same with one another.

As Jesus prepared to wash His disciples' feet, Peter made a seemingly humble remark, "Never shall you wash my feet" (John 13:8). Peter's statement actually revealed his arrogance.

Peter would have to humble himself to the Lord's intention if he would experience the joy of abiding in Christ.

Humility means submitting to one another. Humility requires personal adjustments in order to obey Jesus' word, rather than our traditions (John 13:8-9).

Surrender

The greatest adjustment we must make is to die to ourselves as we surrender to the lordship of Christ. Most of us will probably never endanger our lives by sharing the gospel, but once we are willing to die, the chains of fear that keep us from boldly sharing the gospel can no longer bind us.

Three passages in and around the Upper Room Discourse teach the necessity of death to self as a prerequisite to following Christ: John 12:24, John 13:36-38, and John 15:13-15.

In the chapter immediately prior to the Upper Room Discourse, Jesus prophesied His death, and prepared his disciples for their own difficult road ahead. "Truly, truly, I say to you, unless a grain of wheat falls into the ground and dies, it remains by itself alone; but if it dies it bears much fruit. He who loves his life loses it, and he who hates his life in this world shall keep it to life eternal" (John 12:24-25).

Peter boldly declared his willingness to die for Jesus in the upper room (John 13:37). Later that same night, Peter would deny Jesus three times (John 13:38). Even though he had failed to measure up to his brash prediction, Peter did make a good point. His life and death belonged to Christ. Effective evangelists have already settled the eternity question and are ready to live and die with Christ. Peter, along with the other disciples, would eventually lay down their lives for the gospel.

According to Jesus, true friendship demands a willingness to die. Jesus demonstrated his great love by laying down his life for his friends (John 15:13). Jesus also taught that true friendship is reciprocal, when He said, "You are My friends if you do what I command you" (John 15:14).

As messengers of the gospel we can become one with Christ only as we humble ourselves and surrender completely to Christ. Once a person is humble and willing to die, he is prepared to abide in Christ and experience the greater works that Jesus promised in John 14:12: "Truly, truly, I say to you, he who believes in me, the works that I do, he will do also, and *greater works* than these he will do; because I go to the Father" (italics added for emphasis).

THREE KEYS TO ABIDING IN CHRIST

1. Christ's Walk

Christ's Walk is a walk of prayer. In Luke 5:16, we find, "He often withdrew to deserted places and prayed." And in Luke 6:12, "He went out to the mountain to pray, and spent all night in prayer to God."

Jesus promises to work through those disciples who walk with Him in prayer. "Whatever you ask in My name," Jesus said, "that will I do, so that the Father may be glorified in the Son. If you ask Me anything in My name, I will do it" (John 14:13-14). As we pray according to Christ's word, Christ works through us to fulfill His Great Commission. (John 15:7).

The early disciples prayed when they gathered together, but they also prayed as they went out. For them, prayer was more than a ritual or retreat; it was a continual conversation with their Lord, who accompanied them (Matthew 28:20).

In Any-3, prayer walking is a vital part of the witnessing experience itself. We usually pray together before departing. As we walk, we are praying, "Lord, we surrender ourselves to you. Lead us to those whom you have prepared to hear the gospel. Fill us with the Spirit so we can share the gospel well."

With Any-3, we begin and end with prayer, and pray all along the way. After we have shared the gospel, we ask the person we are witnessing to if we can pray for him or her in Jesus' name. Prayer often results in dramatic answers. Especially when the person comes to faith. Christ reveals His power and presence as if to add an exclamation point to their salvation experience.

2. Christ's Word

Obedience to the word of God is essential to abiding in Christ. "He who has My commands and keeps them is the one who loves Me;" Jesus said, "and he who loves Me will be loved by My Father, and I will love him and will disclose Myself to him" (John 14:22).

Jesus goes on to say, "If you keep My commandments you will abide in My love, just as I have kept the Father's commandments and abide in His love" (John 15:10).

In the book of Acts, we see the disciples living in the word, seeking wisdom from it, and proclaiming it to others. Each time people were filled with the Spirit, in the book of Acts, they proclaimed the word of God with boldness.

In the upper room, Jesus gave at least ten words of instruction for his disciples. Eight of these are commandments, while the other two are bold assumptions.

Ten Words from Christ in the Upper Room

1. "If I then, your Lord and teacher, washed your feet, you also ought to wash one another's feet" (John 13:14).

2. "A new commandment I give to you, that you love one another, even as I have loved you, that you also love one another" (John 13:34; also in 15:12-17).

3. "Do not let your heart be troubled; believe in God, believe also in Me" (John 14:1).

4. "Believe Me that I am in the Father and the Father is in Me" (John 14:11a).

5. "...he who believes in Me, the works that I do, he will do also, and greater works than these he will do; because I go to the Father" (John 14:12).

6. "Abide in Me, and I in you" (John 15:4).

7. "Abide in My love" (John 15:9).

8. "…and you will testify also, because you have been with Me from the beginning" (John 15:27).

9. "…ask and you will receive, so that your joy may be made full" (John 16:24).

10. "In the world you will have tribulation, but take courage; I have overcome the world" (John 16:33).

3. Christ's Works

Christ's Works are those things He does in and through us when we are walking in His Spirit. Abiding in Christ is more than just praying and obeying. The Holy Spirit fills those who do the works of Christ. According to Jesus in the upper room, the primary work to be done by His disciples would be to testify about Him. Jesus promised, "When the Helper comes, whom I will send to you from the Father, that is the Spirit of truth who proceeds from the Father, He will testify about Me, and you will testify also, because you have been with Me from the beginning" (John 15:26-27).

In John 15:8, Jesus said, "My Father is glorified by this: that you produce much fruit and prove to be My disciples." As we abide in Christ, we see Christ's works produced in and through us. Chief among these works is the production of multiplying disciples.

In John 17:4, Jesus prayed to His Father, "I have glorified You on the earth by completing the work You gave Me to do," and then went on to pray for His disciples establishing them in the Word (vs. 8, 14); He prays for them and teaches them to pray (v. 9); He protects them (vs. 11, 15); and He sends them out (v. 18).

Abiding in Christ is the key to doing greater spiritual works. As the disciples abided in Christ through prayer and the word, they did astoundingly significant works. These were the great works recorded in the book of Acts. The disciples planted networks of house churches in Jerusalem, Judea, Samaria and on to the ends of the earth (Acts 1:8) just as Jesus had promised in the upper room.

Christ's Works for His Disciples from the Upper Room

As you seek to be an effective witness for Christ, you might find this acronym helpful to remind you of important aspects of the Spirit-filled life.

Abide in Christ (John 14:16-20; 15:1-8; 17:11, 20-23),

Bold Evangelism (John 15:26-27; 17:20)

Instill Multiplying Discipleship (Bear Increasing Fruit, John 15.2-8)

Develop Churches and Be the Church Together (John 17:15-26)

Equip Leaders (Bear Remaining Fruit, John 15.16; 17:6)

This is the lifestyle of a person who abides in Christ.[21] According to Christ's teaching in the *Greater Works Promise* of John 14:12, those who live in this manner will see even greater works than occurred in the ministry of Christ Himself.

The Greater Works Promise

In John 14:12, Jesus made an earthshaking promise to his disciples. We call it the Greater Works Promise. It has become the theme for the church-planting movement training in the country where I live.

Read the promise slowly to see if you think it applies to you or only to the first-century church. "Truly, truly, I say to you, he who believes in me, the works that I do, he will do also, and greater works than these he will do; because I go to the Father." The promise is for *whoever* believes in Christ. It is a general instruction, not specifically for the apostles but for you and me as well.

Jesus promised two things for those who believed in him: 1) they would do the same kind of works he did, and 2) they would

---

[21] The ABIDE acronym is adapted from a framework introduced by missionary colleagues serving in Asia.

do so to a greater degree. This is not a greater miracle promise. Rather, it is a greater *works* promise. When His disciples meet Jesus' conditions for abiding in him, they participate in the greater works of Christ. This promise was fulfilled for Jesus' first-century disciples in the book of Acts, as the gospel spread from Jerusalem, to Judea, Samaria and the uttermost parts of the earth. When today's disciples abide in Christ and do His works of evangelism, discipleship and church planting they should expect a similar result.

The Greater Works Promise occurs in the Upper Room Discourse. There, Jesus taught his disciples the importance of abiding in Christ. Through abiding in Christ, they would do the greater works promised in John 14:12 and in John 15:1-8. Abiding in Christ is oneness with Him. It is walking in the Spirit, only stated using different terminology. When a person or group of believers is one with Christ, they will share the gospel with fruitfulness. This is exactly what happened in Acts. Each time the disciples were filled with the Spirit, they spoke the word boldly and effectively.

If effective reproducing follow-up is done, an Acts-type church-planting movement can result. The ABIDE acrostic highlights the necessary elements that can contribute to a church-planting movement using Any-3. These elements are shown more clearly in Chapter Fourteen about following up those who are open to the gospel as well as new converts.

12

Any-3 Bridges to Success - Messaging

THERE IS MORE to effective evangelism than a wonderful message, a capable messenger and a good method. Many hidden variables are found in the messaging. Messaging is *how* the messenger shares the gospel. Messaging can result in different degrees of response, even when the gospel is communicated with similar methods to similar peoples.

Evangelistic results improve dramatically when we witness based on what the Bible says rather than what our intuition tells us. Effective evangelists have certain biblically based attitudes and practice certain faith-induced skills that affect their messaging. These messaging qualities appear as the witness walks in the Spirit and shares the gospel. Four such qualities are confidence, expectation, persuasion, and leadership.

WITNESS CONFIDENTLY

"And they were all filled with the Holy Spirit and began to speak the word of God with boldness" (Acts 4:31b). Confident witnesses are bold witnesses. Boldness is not the same as brashness. Boldness is humble yet unapologetic confidence in

Christ's presence. Through the Holy Spirit, we can stand on the truthfulness of the gospel and the authority God has given us to proclaim it to everyone.

When Jesus gave His disciples the Great Commission, He assured them of His authority and his presence. This assurance gave them the confidence to stand before kings as well as ordinary persons, even though they had come from humble, uneducated backgrounds.

"I Have All Authority, So Go!"

Essentially, Jesus was saying, "All authority has been given to Me, and with that authority I am authorizing you to go" (paraphrased from Matthew 28:18). The implication is that everyone who obeys the Great Commission has Christ-given authority to do so. We have the right to share the gospel with kings, paupers and everyone in between.

I know a new believer who was taken to the police station and threatened with 15 years imprisonment if he continued to evangelize. At that very moment, though, instead of remaining silent, he boldly shared the gospel. Two policemen who heard the gospel from him that day came to faith and were baptized.

We are not advocating carelessness or throwing caution to the wind. But we must realize that witnessing encounters do not happen by accident. God orchestrates them. Realize when you are sharing the gospel that the sovereign God has called the meeting, so share the gospel with full confidence.

"I Will Be With You Always"

Leila was an uneducated farmer's wife who grew in confidence as she discovered Christ alongside her as she shared the gospel. Using Any-3, Leila led three other Muslim women to Christ in the radical Muslim province where she lived. She then led her husband to faith, and together they started a house church that has since multiplied into nine groups.

Jesus promised, "I will be with you always" (Matthew 28:20b). When volunteers come to work with us, we can assure them of one thing: "You will experience Christ's presence." He promised it to us, so we confidently promise it to those who go out to share the gospel. Those who intentionally share the gospel do experience Christ's presence. The Lord delights in connecting prepared witnesses with those He is preparing to hear the gospel. This is why it is not unusual for volunteers with minimal training to lead Muslims to faith and even start churches.

Joseph was sharing the gospel with his Muslim friend, Emir, when Emir received a text message from his religious teacher. The text message said, "Today, someone will come and reveal truth to you." Emir showed Joseph the text message along with the goose bumps on his arm. After listening to Joseph's Any-3 message, Emir had to agree, "Only through a sacrifice can our sins be forgiven."

Any-3 Dreaming

As part of a seminary master's degree class, we trained nine students in Any-3 evangelism. The students were initially reluctant to try the approach, but because it was an assignment, they did it. When they shared their experiences the next day, the results were amazing. The most resistant member of the class was a man named Eric, and Eric had led the head of a household to faith. Another student named Juan was moved to tears as he shared his experience. He said, "The Muslim man to whom I witnessed did not seem surprised that I was sharing the gospel with him. The previous week, he had had a dream about Jesus. So when I shared with him, he immediately accepted Christ. He then shared the gospel with his wife." Juan wept as he confessed how he had doubted the gospel's power to save Muslims.

On a different occasion, a missionary and his translator traveled with two mission volunteers to the place where they intended to practice Any-3. On the way, they prayed, "Lord, while these people sleep tonight, visit them with dreams. Connect us with those who are dreaming and let them be persons of peace who will enable the gospel to spread in their area." The next morning, one of the mission volunteers, a middle-aged man named Tom, and his translator accidently went down the wrong road where they met a Muslim named Mehmet who invited them into his home along with several family members and neighbors. As Tom began to share the gospel, Mehmet interrupted, "Last night, I dreamed that two people came to my house. One spoke the local language and the other did not." That morning, two of the persons in Mehmet's home accepted Christ.

The Holy Spirit precedes, accompanies and fills Christ's disciples with boldness as they share the gospel. Christ's presence is most evident when we obey the Great Commission. Every time the disciples were filled with the Holy Spirit in Acts, they spoke the word of God with boldness. You cannot fake confidence; it is the fruit of sharing the gospel while abiding in Christ.

Be confident, because God has made you a capable minister of the new covenant: "Not that we are adequate in ourselves to consider anything as coming from ourselves, but our adequacy is from God, who also made us adequate as servants of a new covenant, not of the letter but of the Spirit; for the letter kills, but the Spirit gives life" (2 Corinthians 3:5-6).

These have been the foundational verses of my ministry ever since I surrendered my life to Christ. By the grace of God, I am a capable minister of the gospel and so are you.

To help build your confidence, take the following actions. First, memorize Matthew 28:18-20 and 2 Corinthians 3:5-6 and review these verses daily. Next, pray daily for the filling of the Holy Spirit as you share the gospel. Also, practice God's presence as you go out to share the gospel by spontaneously conversing with Jesus along the journey. Finally, share the gospel using Any-3 multiple times each week because, as the method becomes more familiar, your confidence will grow.

WITNESS EXPECTANTLY

"A man scatters seed on the ground; night and day he sleeps and gets up, and the seed sprouts and grows—he does not know how. The soil produces a crop by itself—first the blade, then the head, and then the ripe grain in the head. But as soon as the crop is ready, he sends for the sickle, because harvest has come" (Mark 4:26-28).

In this passage, Mark 4:26-28, Jesus teaches us that God has designed the soil to bear fruit. Once the seed is planted, the soil takes over. Good seed that falls on good soil will bear fruit. This is the principle of sowing and reaping.

Faith is expectation. Faith is believing, and *then* seeing; not seeing and then believing. Faith is believing what God has revealed in His word and acting upon it so what God has promised becomes reality. Do not gauge the possibilities of the next witnessing experience based on previous witnessing experiences. Adjust your witnessing approach based upon what God has revealed through His Word then witness by faith.

God has prepared the soil, and when the gospel is shared, the Spirit continues the work in a willing heart until it results in salvation and sanctification.

Some people will come to faith the first time they hear the gospel. Others will hear the gospel and give their life to Christ in a subsequent follow-up meeting. Some may hear the gospel and not respond, because no one follows up with them. After a period of time, God connects them with someone like you, just so they can respond to the gospel.

The Holy Spirit is convicting the world of sin, righteousness and judgment (John 16:8)

When you witness, even to unresponsive persons, you are never wasting your breath. The Holy Spirit is convicting them of their sin and disbelief. Though they cannot see Jesus with their own eyes, the Spirit is revealing Christ to them. The Spirit is also convicting them of the judgment to come. Knowing that the Spirit works in this way encourages us as we partner with the Spirit and share the gospel expectantly with the lost.

People will respond to the gospel in one of four ways

Jesus' Parable of the Sower (Mark 4:10-20) anticipates the following responses:

1) Some will hear, but will immediately reject it. 2) Others will hear it, and though they initially open their hearts, they will afterwards turn away. 3) Others will hear and open their hearts to the gospel, but will become entangled with other things, and so fail to be fruitful. 4) *But some will hear the word, open their hearts and continue in the faith.* They will also bear multiplying fruit.

Any-3 will help that fruitful person respond to the gospel and become your partner for reaching a people group or city. Should the Lord use you to reach persons of peace, these persons of peace will reach multiple others as they follow the same Any-3 pattern.

One of our Asian partners, a man named Jonas, used Any-3 faithfully in a difficult area without seeing anyone come to Christ for four months. When Jonas did see a breakthrough, the results were astounding. In the initial two-month period when the gospel began spreading, more than 120 persons were baptized and nine discipleship groups were started among his Muslim people group. These were the first known believers among this unreached people group. After 13 months, more than 400 new believers had been baptized.

"Connect us"

Throughout the practice of Any-3, we continually pray, "Lord, connect us with people who are open to the gospel." When we are ready to share the gospel, God connects us to the right people, in the right places at just the right times.

Caleb, a college student on a short-term mission trip, joined a career missionary named Pete to do Any-3 evangelism in a public park. The two walked together while praying, "Lord, connect us with someone who is open to your word. Fill us with your Spirit so we can share the gospel." After a short while, the pair were joined by a seemingly radical Muslim man. After walking with him for a while, they sat together and began sharing the gospel with him. Two hours later, the man came to faith in Christ. After experiencing this, Caleb said, "I have never seen anything like this." Pete responded, "I often see this sort of thing happen. I am always amazed by what God does, but I am rarely surprised anymore."

God is calling them

Who are these Muslims who are coming to faith through Any-3 evangelism? Some are only nominal in their religion, but others are radical Muslims who have been awakened by the Holy Spirit to realize their hopeless condition. Some of those who respond are Imams, religious leaders in their community. There is no way to predict *who* will be open to the gospel, but there is a clear pattern of *how* they come to faith. They hear the gospel, the Holy Spirit convicts them and draws them to Christ. They surrender to Jesus through repentance, and confess their faith In Christ, and are saved.

WITNESS PERSUASIVELY

"Therefore, knowing the fear of the lord, we persuade men" (1 Corinthians 5:11a).

The apostles witnessed persuasively

The apostles commanded people to repent. "Repent, and each of you be baptized in the name of Jesus Christ for the forgiveness of your sins; and you will receive the gift of the Holy Spirit" Acts 2:38). Peter's Pentecost sermon continues, "And with many other words he solemnly testified and kept on exhorting them, saying, 'Be saved from this perverse generation!'"

In Acts 18:4, Luke says that Paul "reasoned in the synagogue every Sabbath and tried to persuade both Jews and Greeks." Paul used many methods to communicate the gospel, but always he sought to persuade them to come to repentance.

Jesus commanded His followers to make disciples of all peoples (Matthew 28:18-20). In response, Jesus' disciples passionately persuaded people to surrender to Christ and escape the wrath to come.

Today, we prefer less confrontational terms such as "share" the gospel rather than persuade. Witnessing begins with sharing the gospel but does not end there. Proclaiming the gospel requires persuasion from the witness.

Some Christians wrongly conclude that because God is sovereign, it is enough to merely "share" the gospel. Their role in evangelism becomes passive because they are not certain that God wills each lost person to be saved, even though the Bible insists that God is "not wishing for any to perish but for all to come to repentance" (2 Peter 3:9; 1 Timothy 2:4). They intentionally do not try to persuade people to follow Christ, so as to not inappropriately impinge on God's sovereign right to call only those whom He has chosen. In the Bible, the apostles passionately persuaded people to come to Christ, realizing that those who responded were the called of God (Acts 13:48). God, who is sovereign in all things, has called us to proclaim the gospel persuasively.

Sincerity demands persuasion

When the witness sincerely believes the gospel is good news for perishing sinners, he will share it persuasively. A sincere witness cannot take a passive position when the eternal destiny of people is at stake.

Effective persuasion, as far as the gospel is concerned, cannot be self-generated. Self-generated persuasion reeks of insincerity. Images of traveling snake oil salesmen and exaggerated infomercials come to mind when 'insincere persuasion' is mentioned. A true message proclaimed with heartfelt sincerity persuades people to consider it.

In the Parable of the Great Banquet (Luke 14:16-24), Jesus taught, "Go out into the highways and along the hedges, and *compel* them to come in, so that my house may be filled"

(14:23, italics added). Through this parable, Jesus emphasizes the role of persuasion by using the word "compel." He wanted His disciples to understand that an invitation to the banquet feast of the Messiah must be communicated persuasively.

Persuasion is calling people to respond to the Holy Spirit's conviction. It may not require 'loudness.' Many loud, brash people are not very persuasive. Persuasion means convincing a person's heart with the truth of the gospel. Teaching expands the mind, but persuasion opens the heart. "And have mercy on some, who are doubting; save others, snatching them out of the fire; and on some have mercy with fear...." (Jude 22-23a).

LEAD PEOPLE TO SURRENDER

"And Jesus said unto them, 'Follow Me, and I will make you become fishers of men" (Mark 1:17).

Effective evangelism is more than sharing the gospel; it is *leading* people to Christ. Jesus led people to Himself. He urged them, "Follow me." People do not just *find* Jesus. Christ calls them to Himself, and someone leads them to the Savior. Like the woman at the well, we bring people to Christ. "Come see a man who told me all the things that I have done," the Samaritan woman said (John 4:29a). "Come" implies going somewhere together, and it signals that the inviter will lead them to that destination.

Effective evangelists work in partnership with the Holy Spirit to lead people to faith. Consider the case of Paul's witness to Lydia in Philippi. Acts 16:14 says, "the Lord opened her heart to respond to Paul's message." The Holy Spirit is doing His part, our part is to lead the lost to faith. Leadership is often the single quality that differentiates those who bring people to faith from those who rarely bring people to faith.

Leading a potential convert to Christ may require casting a vision for him of what his new life in Christ would be like. You may tell him, "Hundreds of people like you have surrendered themselves to Christ. Followers of Christ can worship in their own homes. New followers of Jesus often lead their spouses, children, and friends to Christ and become a house church together."

As you lead them to Christ, you can pose clarifying questions such as, "Do you believe the message I have been sharing with you? If so, it is time to submit yourself to Christ, isn't it?" Help them know what steps they need to take by saying, "The way people usually profess faith in Christ is through a prayer." Walk with them to faith by offering to lead them in a prayer to receive Christ. Show them what to do next and follow up with them to do it.

THE HOLY SPIRIT'S WORK

"And He, when He comes, will convict the world concerning sin, and righteousness, and judgment" (John 16:8).

The messaging qualities of confidence, expectation, persuasion and leadership are only effective because of the powerful work of the Holy Spirit all around us. It is He who connects us with persons of peace and it is He who convicts them of their need for salvation.

Describing His own ministry, Jesus said, "...the Son of Man has come to seek and to save that which was lost" (Luke 19:10). Jesus' purpose statement in this verse is from the passage where Zacchaeus pursues Jesus by climbing a tree in order to get a glimpse of him. Upon closer examination, we see that Jesus was actually pursuing Zacchaeus. Jesus called him by name, and accompanied him to his house, where Zacchaeus repented and was saved (Luke 19:9). In the same way, God is seeking to save men, women, boys and girls throughout the world.

Regardless of whether or not the person to whom we witness responds positively to the gospel, the very fact that we are witnessing to them is evidence that God is pursuing him or her. In Colossians 4:3, Paul encouraged the church to "...pray also for us that God may open a door to us for the message, to speak the mystery of the Messiah...." If we pray beforehand that God will connect us with people whom He is preparing, He will do it. I often tell the person I am witnessing to that I prayed that God would connect me with someone that He is preparing and that he or she is that person.

God desires their salvation (1 Timothy 2:4, 2 Peter 3:9), paid for it on the cross (1 Timothy 2:6), and now has the bearer of good news in their presence. Once we have shared the gospel and drawn the net, we will see the extent of the Holy Spirit's pursuit of them through their response.

Jesus instructed his disciples to be on the lookout for where the Holy Spirit had been at work convicting men and women of their need for salvation. In Luke 10, Jesus sent 72 disciples into the villages of Galilee telling them, "And whatever city or village you enter, inquire who is worthy in it, and stay at his house until you leave that city" (Matthew 10:11).

These "worthy" persons were known as "persons of peace." Persons of peace are typically the first believers who go on to reach their *oikos* (family and friends) and plant the first churches in their respective communities. Persons of peace not only hear and receive the gospel; they also become catalysts to spread the gospel to their family, neighbors, and friends.

Jesus encountered many persons of peace in his own ministry. Nicodemus (John 3), Zacchaeus (Luke 19), the Samaritan woman (John 4), and Joseph of Arimathea (John 19) were all persons of peace. We should expect to find persons of peace as well.

Persons of peace appear throughout the New Testament as Jesus' disciples followed his evangelism pattern. We see examples of persons of peace in Lydia of Thyatira who "opened her heart to respond to the things spoken by Paul" after which her whole household was baptized (Acts 16:14-15), and the Philippian jailer in Acts 16:19-34 who cried out to Paul and Silas, "Sirs, what must I do to be saved?" After hearing the gospel, the Bible says, "...immediately he was baptized, he and all who were in his house."

Wherever we go, we can know that the Holy Spirit has preceded us. And we can be certain that there are persons of peace awaiting us. The only sure way to identify a person of peace is to share the gospel with him or her and see how they respond. When we find a person of peace, we know that the Holy Spirit is at work and that is the surest pathway to effective ministry.

Part Three
ANY-3 FOR EVERYONE

13

The Any-3 Workshop

THREE DAYS BEFORE writing this chapter, I led an Any-3 workshop for 32 Asian partners. During the first evening practicum, those we trained shared the gospel nearly 70 times. When they returned for the final session, they had led ten persons to Christ, more than half of them Muslims.

Any-3 one-day workshops are the way we are training others to initiate and multiply church-planting movements. After a 4-6 hour training session, we go out in the evening to practice what we've learned. During this evening practicum we almost always see at least one person come to faith. Invariably, workshop participants experience Christ's joy and presence as they share their faith and obey the Great Commission.

Whenever we share the gospel, but especially when people respond to it, the result is both praise to God, and inexpressible joy for the witness. During one workshop, a participant admitted, "I used to share the gospel, but it became drudgery. I want evangelism to feel like a hobby again, something I deeply enjoy." After sharing the gospel that evening, she returned with great joy. Yes, evangelism is a sobering responsibility but Christians should enjoy it —Jesus did, the first-century disciples did (Luke 10:17-21), and so can you.

This chapter is written to train you to equip others in Any-3. I am confident that you have learned enough in this book already to implement Any-3 in your own community, even if you are not able to join a workshop. Recently, an Asian partner reported this very thing. He had read the Any-3 training material, but had not yet participated in a workshop. Putting what he learned from the training material into practice, he proceeded to lead four people to faith in the very resistant area where he lived. We believe you will be able to do the same. And with the help of this chapter, you will be well equipped to train others as well.

ANY-3 LEARNING PLAN

The Any-3 workshop consists of three parts. Part One: Learning Any-3, Part Two: Practicing Any-3, and Part Three: Accountability and Celebration.

Session preparation for the workshop leader: Familiarize yourself with the content of this book before you lead an Any-3 workshop. You will frequently be directed back to the chapter content of this book as you lead your trainees. Read over the workshop program below and practice, in your mind, how you would lead trainees through each of the three parts.

Session preparation for trainees: Before they arrive for the workshop, have the trainees read John 4. Ask them to try to identify Jesus' motivations in John 4:28-42 that will compel a Christian into the harvest fields.

Activity-oriented learning: Any-3 workshops are not long (usually 4 - 6 hours), but they are deliberately activity oriented. When learning the Any-3 witnessing method, participants practice each step with a partner. After each step is taught, it gets "caught" as pairs practice with one another.

Practice does not make perfect, but it prepares trainees and gives them confidence. The more they practice, the more they "get it." Practice beforehand gives participants the competence and confidence they need to share the gospel that evening with someone they have just met.

PART ONE: LEARNING ANY-3

Segment 1: Motivations   *.5 hour - 1 hour*

Segment Objective: Familiarization with the motivations for entering the harvest field found in John 4:28-36.

Compare your trainees' findings with the five motivations found in Chapter Nine in this book.

1) Lead the trainees to see the biblical basis for each of the five motivations as described in Chapter Nine.

2) In small groups of 3-4, have trainees discuss how each motivation impacts witnessing.

3) Finally, pair up and test one another on the five motivations for witnessing.

Segment 2: Any-3 Insights   *.5 hour - 1 hour*

Segment Objective: Familiarization with the *Any-3 Insights* described in Chapter Seven.

Briefly describe for your trainees, each of the five *Any-3 Insights*. Solicit from your trainees answers to the following "Insight Questions," being careful to draw out the "Points to Emphasize" listed below.

Intentional

Insight Question: Why did Jesus *have* to go to Samaria?

Point to Emphasize: Jesus did not have to go for physical or logistical reasons, but for reasons of obedience.

Insight Question: Was Jesus' witnessing encounter at the well planned or spontaneous?

Point to Emphasize: Point out how Any-3-style evangelism *is* planned but feels spontaneous because of the Spirit's work.

Informal

Insight Question: Was Jesus' witnessing encounter formal or informal?

Point to Emphasize: Jesus' witnessing encounter was informal. Have them rate the experience on a formality scale, with 1 being least formal and 10 being most formal. Point out that the society in Jesus' day would not allow formal interaction between a man and a woman.

Interactive

Insight Question: Did Jesus preach to the woman or talk interactively with her?

Point to Emphasize: Jesus spoke interactively with the woman. Point out that Jesus spoke seven times and the woman spoke six times during the conversation.

Initiative

Insight Question: Who guided the conversation between Jesus and the woman?

Point to Emphasize: Though we may begin a conversation by listening and asking questions, we do not end there. Guiding or driving the conversation toward the gospel is vital to effective witnessing. Read aloud Jesus' conversation with the woman in John 4:7-26. Ask participants to say, "Drive" each time Jesus took initiative to turn the conversation a different way.

Introducing the Messiah

Insight Question: What was the most important thing Jesus wanted to communicate to this woman in John 4:25-26?

Point to Emphasize: Jesus wanted her to know that He was the Messiah.

Insight Question: What does it mean for us to introduce the Messiah?

Points to Emphasize: Have one of your trainees read aloud Luke 24:44-49, and then answer the Insight Question: *What is the most important thing we can communicate to a lost person?* Now have them read 1 Corinthians 1:17, and do the same.

Segment 3: Mastering Any-3   *2.5 - 3.5 hours*

Segment Objective: For trainees to gain confidence and competence in the five steps of Any-3 as described in Chapter Two.

Say out loud each of the five Any-3 steps: *Get connected. Get to a God conversation. Get to lostness. Get to the gospel. Get to a decision.*

Have your trainees repeat each of these steps after you. Then have your trainees say them together with you. Repeat this activity.

Discuss with your trainees how each of the five Any-3 steps appear in Jesus' witness to the woman at the well in John 4.

Step One: Get Connected (15 minutes)

Discuss how Jesus got connected with the woman at the well (John 4:7).

Point to Emphasize: For this practice, limit your getting connected to 3-4 minutes building around the two questions: "How are you?" and "Who are you?"

Transition from *Get Connected* to *Get to a God Conversation* by using the following transition question.

Transition Question: "Are you Hindu, Muslim, Buddhist, or Christian?" or "What religion do you follow?"

At this point, you may hear one of the three responses that could derail your progress. Instead, take this opportunity to practice driving or redirecting the conversation toward the next step in your Any-3 witness.

THREE COMMON RESPONSES

Response #1:
"I am a Muslim, but I believe all religions are good."

Any-3 Reply: Yes, most religions are alike, aren't they? We are all trying to please God, and we are trying to get our sins forgiven. We are all sinners aren't we?

Response #2:
"I am a Muslim (then silence)."

Any-3 Reply: Most religions are alike, aren't they? We are all trying to please God, and we are trying to get our sins forgiven. We are all sinners aren't we?

Response #3:
"I am a Muslim, how about you?"

Any-3 Reply: I was raised in a religious home. I used to try hard to be a good person, so I could please God. However, though I tried to be good, I was never quite good enough. God is in heaven and is holy, but we on the earth are unholy. Through our religion, we try to please God with our good works, but it is never enough. We climb, then fall. Climb, then fall. It's frustrating, isn't it? Most religions are alike aren't they? We are all trying to please God, to get our sins forgiven.

If you find yourself in response #3, you can use the "Human Effort Cannot Replace Sins" illustration found in Appendix B.

Now get into pairs and practice transitioning from *Getting Connected* to *Getting to a God Conversation* with one person serving as the Any-3 witness and the other a Muslim. Then reverse roles.

Step Two: Get to a God Conversation (30-45 minutes)

Point to emphasize: If they have not already said it themselves, steer the conversation to the observation that "Most religions are alike, aren't they? Most religions are trying to please God, and pay off our sin debt."

Then say: "We are all sinners aren't we? Even good people sin. Sinning is easy, but paying off our sin debt to God is much more difficult, isn't it?"

Transition Question: "In your religion, what are you doing to pay off your sin debt?" or "In your religion, what are you doing to please God?"

A Muslim will usually list the following: daily prayers, giving alms, and fasting during Ramadan. They might also list the pilgrimage to Mecca or the Muslim confession of faith.

Discuss and demonstrate *Get to a God Conversation*. Have participants practice *Getting to a God Conversation* in pairs.

Step Three: Get to Lostness (30-45 minutes)

Summarize what you have heard from your Muslim friend by repeating back to him or her what he has said: "So, you are trying to pay off your sins by praying five times daily, giving alms, fasting during Ramadan, and taking the pilgrimage to Mecca."

Now ask these three questions:

1) "Are your sins forgiven yet?"

2) "When will your sins be forgiven?" and

3) "On judgment day, do you know that your sins will be forgiven?"

Transition Statement: "What I believe is different. I know my sins are forgiven."

Get into pairs and practice *Getting to Lostness* with one person serving as the Any-3 witness and the other a Muslim. Then reverse roles.

Step Four: Get to the Gospel (1-1.5 hours)

Tell *The First and Last Sacrifice Story* from Chapter Six. Don't let the length of this story overwhelm you. It is really only the Adam and Eve story with a brief story about Jesus woven into it. You can divide the story into three parts and a conclusion to make it easier for your trainees to learn.

Part one of the story begins with the phrase, "Jesus, the Word of God, was in Heaven with God from the beginning" and ends with, "Do you know why Jesus said, 'I must die?'" Part two begins with, "The answer is in the *Taurat* (what Muslims call the books of Moses)" and ends with "All of our forefathers offered sacrifices to have their sins forgiven: Adam and Eve, Cain and Abel, Noah, Abraham, Moses, David, etc." Part three of the story begins with, "Then Jesus came, like I told you earlier" and ends with, "The Bible tells us that if we surrender ourselves to Jesus as Lord and believe that He paid for our sins through his sacrifice and was raised from the dead, our sins will be forgiven. The conclusion to the story is: And that is why I know my sins are forgiven."

Transition Question: "It makes sense, doesn't it, that we cannot pay off our own sins but that God made a way for our sins to be forgiven through Jesus' sacrifice?"

Have your trainees break into pairs and practice telling *The First and Last Sacrifice Story* one-third at a time. After each participant tells one-third of the story, switch and let the other participant tell the next third, alternating until the story is completed. Then repeat the process.

Step Five: Get to a Decision

Transition Question: "Do you believe that Jesus died as a sacrifice for our sins and was raised from the dead?"

Discuss and demonstrate from Chapter Twelve's "Lead People to Surrender to Christ" how to lead someone to Christ. Have participants practice drawing the net in pairs.

Gauge the level of openness, based upon the answer to your two *Get to a Decision* questions. He or she may answer: *Yes, No, or I do not know.*

1. If he says "Yes" (If he believes the gospel):

    a. Make sure he understands, by asking, "So, you believe that Jesus died for our sins and was raised from the dead?"

    b. Read or quote Romans 10:9-10.

    c. Clarify that the qualifications for salvation are surrendering to Jesus as Lord, and believing the gospel.

    d. Lead him to faith by saying, "The way that people usually surrender themselves to Jesus is through prayer. How about this, I'll lead you in a prayer to surrender yourself to Jesus."

2. If he says, "No." (If he's not open to the gospel)

    a. Review the gospel briefly, then feel free to change the subject.

3. If he says, "I do not know," then he may be open to the gospel, but not yet ready to receive Christ.

    a. If time allows, immediately tell the Cain and Abel story, emphasizing that God received the animal sacrifice.

    b. If time does not allow for immediate follow-up, ask

if you can get back together within the following day or two to study with him one of the Old Testament sacrifice stories.

   c. Ask permission to pray for him in Jesus' name. Pray for his personal needs and for Jesus to affirm the gospel to him.

Now, get into pairs and practice drawing the net.

Segment 4: Master The Transitions   .5 hour

Memorizing the five steps of Any-3 is surprisingly easy. Mastering the transition statements and questions can be more challenging. Getting from one step of Any-3 to the next is vital for effectiveness; learning the transitions will make it much easier.

So pair up with a partner and practice moving through the five steps with these transition statements.

Step One: Get Connected

Transition #1: "Are you Hindu, Muslim, Buddhist, or Christian?"

Step Two: Get to God

Transition #2: "In your religion, what are you doing to pay off your sin debt?" or "In your religion, what are you doing to please God?"

Step Three: Get to Lostness

Transition #3: "What I believe is different; I know my sins are forgiven, because God himself has made a way for our sins to be forgiven."

Step Four: Get to the Gospel

Transition #4: "It makes sense, doesn't it, that we cannot pay off our own sins but that God made a way for our sins to be forgiven through Jesus' sacrifice?"

Step Five: Get to a Decision

Transition #5: "Do you believe that Jesus died as a sacrifice for our sins and was raised from the dead?"

Now that the training is complete, your trainees are ready to put what they have learned into practice.

PART TWO: PRACTICING ANY-3

Part two of the Any-3 workshop is where your training turns into action. In this portion of the workshop, your trainees will go out into the community to practice Any-3. It is usually best, though not essential, for trainees to go out in pairs. Before they go out, ask them to identify persons they would like to visit, or places where they can prayer walk with the aim of engaging in Any-3 conversations.

Session activities:

Assign trainees to go out for the day or evening to use Any-3 to witness to at least two persons. Remind trainees that they are each to share the entire gospel and ask the person if they believe it.

Schedule the time and location for the final part of your workshop -- Part Three: Accountability and Celebration.

Pray for trainees and send them out to proclaim the gospel Any-3 style. Remind them to be continually in prayer that God will connect them with someone whom He is preparing to hear the gospel.

PART THREE: ACCOUNTABILITY
AND CELEBRATION

Your Any-3 Workshop is not complete without Part Three: "Accountability and Celebration." When done correctly, this part of the workshop will encourage faithfulness and build faith for future Any-3 efforts. You should schedule Part Three on the day or evening following Part Two's Practicing Any-3.

Session activities:

When the trainees return from their Any-3 witnessing experience, write the five steps of Any-3 evangelism on one side of the whiteboard, and the five characteristics or "Any-3 Insights" (*Intentional, Informal, Interactive, Initiative, Introducing the Messiah*) on the other side.

Ask the trainees to report on their progress in and through each of the five steps of Any-3. Take time to enjoy their adventure. Celebrate their successes and encourage them in their shortcomings.

As each trainee shares his or her experiences with Any-3, lead the group to analyze their report according to the five "Any-3 Insights" (*Intentional, Informal, Interactive, Initiative, Introducing the Messiah*).

Of course it was *Intentional* because they were fulfilling their assignment. Ask them, how many people heard the gospel because they intentionally shared? Were their witnessing experiences *Informal?* Ask the following questions: To whom did they witness? And where did they witness? Were there experiences *Interactive* or preachy? Were they able to take appropriate *Initiative* in order to drive the conversation toward the gospel? What obstacles did they face?

Finally, did they *Introduce the Messiah?* How many of them actually shared the gospel with someone? Did anyone invite Jesus into his or her life as Savior and Lord? Celebrate with those who shared the gospel. Encourage those who haven't yet shared the gospel to do so before the day ends. Celebrate anyone who came to new life in Christ

The Any-3 "Accountability and Celebration" session should also introduce the importance of follow-up with those who professed faith or were open to the gospel. The next chapter, "Follow-up for a CPM," describes how we do a follow-up. This method allows us to get to a new church start with a new convert rather than taking him to church with us. You may want to schedule some additional time with your Any-3 trainees just to walk through the follow-up process with them.

14
Follow-up for a Church-Planting Movement

NEXT TO LEADING someone to faith in Christ, follow-up is the most important element that determines whether the new believer will remain a single convert, or become the seed of a new church. In fact, the new believer could be a person whom God uses to start a church-planting movement.

In our own emerging church-planting movement, we use a follow-up discipleship plan that follows the ABIDE acrostic introduced to you in Chapter Eight. The steps we follow from new believer to church-planting movement are: **A**bide in Christ, **B**old Evangelism (Any-3), **I**nstill Multiplication, **D**evelop Churches, and **E**quip Leaders.

Let's review each aspect of the **ABIDE** acrostic.

Abiding In Christ

We abide in Christ as we practice Christ's walk, Christ's word and Christ's works. The prerequisites for abiding in Christ are a spirit of humility and a willingness to die for the sake of Christ.

Bold Evangelism

Any-3 is bold evangelism. We use bold evangelism with persons who say "yes" to the gospel, or who express openness to learning more about the gospel. Let's first look at how we follow up with open, but not yet believing, persons. Afterwards, we will examine how to follow up with new converts.

Follow-Up for Open Persons

We invite persons who are open to the gospel to meet with us twice a week to learn more about the gospel, using sacrifice stories from the Old Testament. In our church-planting movement, we have adapted the discipleship and evangelism training method called "Training for Trainers," or T4T, that was developed by one of our missionary colleagues in Asia.[22] Much of what you read in this chapter is drawn from that fruitful program of training multiplying disciples.

T4T begins with the first follow-up visit and continues through the establishing of multiplying discipleship communities, or churches. There are three objectives each time we meet: 1) Encourage them and hold them accountable, 2) Teach them a new Bible story or lesson, discussing it with the use of interactive questions, and 3) Pray for one another and send them out. The following paragraphs explain what that looks like.

First, we hold them accountable. In the first follow-up meeting we commend them for their willingness to come and learn more about God. We then ask them, "Have you shared *The First and Last Sacrifice Story* that I told you with anyone else?" During our Any-3 witnessing encounter, we did not give them an assignment to share the story, but it is helpful to see if they shared it without prompting. Beginning with the first follow-up visit, we review the story with them and challenge them to share the story with five other persons. The next time we meet we ask them, "With whom did you share the story?" and "How did it go?" If they struggled, we encourage them, and review the story once again. If they succeeded, we celebrate their faithfulness. This model

---

[22] The T4T discipleship approach is thoroughly explained in Steve Smith and Ying Kai's book, *T4T: A Discipleship Re-Revolution* (Monument, CO: WIGTake Resources, 2011). A brief introduction to T4T is found on the website: www. T4TOnline.org.

of encouragement, practice and accountability instills an active pattern of obedience to God's word.

After they have proven faithful in sharing *The First and Last Sacrifice Story*, we teach them a new story. We follow *The First and Last Sacrifice Story* with a retelling of the Adam and Eve story with some additional information. The Adam and Eve story is foundational because it equips a person to share the gospel with others, even if they have not yet fully accepted it for themselves.

In the second telling of the Adam and Eve story add the story of Cain and Able. In each subsequent meeting, you can add another Old Testament sacrifice story. Each of these stories culminates in a gospel presentation. The other sacrifice stories include Noah, Abraham, Moses (Passover) and Moses (Law). After you relate each story, use six questions to stimulate thoughtful interaction and to model the way new believers will also study the Bible in your absence.[23]

1) First, ask them: Can you retell the story? They might be a little apprehensive at first, but with some encouragement, they will be able to do it. After they retell the story, ask the following questions:

2) What do we learn about the Lord from this story?

3) What is the most interesting part of this story to you?

4) Why is this story still relevant?

5) What must we obey in this story?

6) Who are five people to whom you will tell this story before our next meeting?[24]

The main point of each of the initial follow-up stories is that a sacrifice was offered because this is what God required. When discussing each story, share the gospel again. This fits well with the fourth question, "Why is this story *still* relevant?" The story

---

[23] This process can be done with a single individual or with a group.

[24] In high persecution settings, you will want to discuss and pray with your trainee in advance how to share in a bold, yet wise manner.

is still relevant because God teaches us that the forgiveness of sins requires a blood sacrifice. And Jesus Christ is the Lamb of God, whose own sacrifice has paid for the world's sins.

Finally, we pray for the person in Jesus' name. We pray for his personal and family needs. We also pray that God will guide him into truth and protect him from error. Praying that God will help him tell the story to the five people whom he designated also will encourage him to follow through with the commitment.

Should the person profess faith in Christ at any time, you have already demonstrated a pattern for each subsequent meeting: 1) Celebrating faithfulness, 2) Studying a new passage, and 3) Sending him out. The three-part pattern will develop into a more mature pattern with time, but these three essential elements of a weekly meeting are already present in the first follow-up visit.

When the person is ready to repent of sin and turn to Christ, lead the new believer to pray to surrender himself or herself to Christ. Whenever a person professes faith, seek to baptize him or her as soon as possible, according to the Great Commission (Matthew 28:18-20).

Now, let's take a look at the process we use for follow-up of new converts.

Follow-Up Process for New Converts

The first follow-up meeting takes place immediately after conversion and focuses on the Ethiopian eunuch story (Acts 8:25-40). After discussing the story, explain that baptism symbolizes the death and resurrection of Jesus Christ (Romans 6:4), and is done in obedience to the Great Commission (Matthew 28:18-20). Follow the Acts baptismal pattern.[25]

---

[25] Baptism in Acts follows a pattern that can be remembered with the vowels A, E, I, O, U: **A**fter their profession of faith in Jesus Christ, **E**very person who professed faith was baptized, **I**mmersion was always the practiced form, The **O**ne who reached them, was typically the one who baptized them, and it was **U**rgent (immediate) as a demonstration of obedience. Implementation of the Acts formula is vital to facilitate generational transfer of the gospel and baptism.

In your second meeting with the new believer, teach, discuss and help them to learn the story about fruits of repentance in the Ephesian church (Acts 19:13-20). The supporting verse is 1 Peter 1:14-16. The objective of this meeting is for the new convert to break sinful patterns of his or her pre-conversion life, including any occultist practices.[26]

In the third post-conversion meeting teach, discuss and learn the passage John 15:1-8. This is the first time a Bible passage, rather than a story, is used as lesson material. The objective of this meeting is to introduce the three keys to abiding in Christ: Christ's walk (continual prayer), Christ's word (obedience to Christ's commandments), and Christ's works (doing as Jesus did). You can introduce the first memory verse in this meeting as well, John 15:5.[27]

Instill Multiplying Discipleship

Whereas the initial follow-up lessons focus on the new convert's relationship with God, the lessons in the "Instill Multiplying Discipleship" section are focused outward. These lessons come immediately after the initial follow-up lessons. They are designed to prepare the new convert to reach their family members, friends, and other relationships, and potentially a new church-planting stream.

First Lesson: Study the Cornelius Story (Acts 10:1-48) using the six-question approach from the follow-up for the open people section. Memorize 2 Timothy 2:2 together.

---

[26] We emphasize repentance when inviting a person to surrender to Jesus Christ as Lord in the "Get to a Decision" phase of evangelism. We reaffirmed repentance in the second follow-up visit. This lesson has proven very beneficial to help Animists and Spiritists break from their pre-conversion practices.

[27] After the steps of following up a new convert are completed, the new convert should master the remaining sacrifice stories from the "Follow Up Open People" section if he has not already done so. This will equip him to reach, gather, and lead a group in his community. Continue to meet with the new convert weekly, and later bi-weekly in order to mentor him or her in the process of evangelism and starting house churches.

Make "Oikos Lists" of family, friends, and relationships like the ones on the next page. Pray for the salvation of those on the lists and for guidance to know with whom to share the gospel using Any-3, which will be taught as the next objective.

Second Lesson: Teach them to use *The First and Last Sacrifice Story* (found in Chapter Six) to share the gospel.

From their *Oikos Lists,* ask the new convert to prayerfully identify five people to whom the Spirit leads him or her. Lead the new convert to pray for those persons and make plans to witness to them using Any-3. The witness should invite open, responsive persons to study the sacrifice stories twice weekly, following the same process that was used to reach and follow up with him.

Third Lesson: Arrange a follow-up meeting to evaluate the results and to further master the Any-3 method. Once the new convert has a good grasp of Any-3, proceed to the fourth lesson.

Fourth Lesson: Study Acts 16:22-34 and teach three vital factors for reaching their *oikos* (family, friends and relationships). The first factor is the good news of the gospel. When they share the gospel, the Holy Spirit will convict people of their sins and many will become believers. The second factor is their changed lives. When people witness positive changes occur in their lives, and hear their personal testimonies, they will be drawn to Jesus. The third factor is the power of Jesus Christ. The new believer can set a pattern of praying for people in Jesus' name. Praying for solutions to problems in the household, illnesses, temptations, etc. invites Jesus to reveal Himself in their lives.

OIKOS LISTS

Family

1._____   6._____

2._____   7._____

3._____   8._____

4._____   9._____

5._____   10._____

Friends

1._____   6._____

2._____   7._____

3._____   8._____

4._____   9._____

5._____   10._____

Relationships

1._____   6._____

2._____   7._____

3._____   8._____

4._____   9._____

5._____   10._____

Develop Multiplying House Churches

Instructions for Developing Study Groups Into House Churches

Encourage all new disciples to model the training process with a new group that they have started while still attending their original group. After the initial follow-up stage, group meetings should occur weekly, allowing time for the new convert to start a new group as well.

As new disciples progress in their understanding and practice of and obedience to the biblical stories, the content of the weekly follow-up meeting takes shape as a house church meeting, taking definitive form as those participating in the group are baptized. Each meeting still follows the three-part format: 1) Encourage and hold them accountable, 2) Teaching them a new Bible story or lesson and discussing it using interactive and obedience-based questions, and 3) praying for them and sending them out. The following paragraphs explain what that looks like.

First Third of the Meeting

The order of elements in the first third of the house church meeting can vary, but they should always include encouragement and accountability. Mutually encourage one another in the Christian walk. Ask one another whether they were obedient to the previous lesson, as well as whether or not they have been teaching it to others. Ask one another who has shared the gospel with 3-5 people since the previous meeting. Pray for another and encourage one another. When someone demonstrates obedience to Christ, celebrate their faithfulness. Casting a vision for faithfulness is also essential in the first third. In our own movement, we recite together a short vision statement: "The gospel for each person and a house church in every village of our people."

Whether you sing or recite psalms together may vary depending on your security situation. This praise time can occur in the first or second third of the meeting. In our movement, we include the following profession of faith:

Jesus Christ is Lord, to the glory of God the Father (Philippians 2:11b). He wants all men to be saved and to come to the knowledge of the truth. For there is one God and one mediator also between God and men, the man Christ Jesus, who gave himself as a ransom for all .(1 Timothy 2:4-6a)

Second Third of the Meeting

The second third of the meeting is primarily interactive Bible study. Though we use oral Bible stories in the initial follow-up sessions, new groups very quickly begin studying passages directly from the Bible, assuming that at least one person in the group can read. The six-question set basically remains the same. However, instead of retelling the story the first question becomes, "What is this passage about?" Also, for the final question we may request the disciple to share the story with three persons, rather than the five he or she will witness to later.

Final Third of the Meeting

The final third of the meeting includes three activities: practicing the lesson, setting goals and a commissioning prayer. The purpose of practicing is so the attendees can master the lesson they will teach others. Training often includes a memory verse. Attendees set goals for how many persons and to whom they will teach the lesson and share the gospel before the next meeting. Finally, participants pray for one another, commissioning themselves back into the world to teach and share the gospel.

Over subsequent weeks, the follow-up discipleship group takes on more and more characteristics of a discipleship-based church. As the group completes the initial four lessons, they can transition into a 20-lesson study aimed at helping them mature as disciples and as a church.

Ten Stages of Spiritual Growth for House Churches

The goal of every follower of Christ and every church is to become spiritually mature. We use 20 lessons to guide disciples and emerging house churches through ten stages of spiritual development. The ten stages of spiritual growth mirror the growth process of the physical body, with one exception. The first stage of physical growth is birth, but the first stage in spiritual growth is death — that is identifying with the death of Jesus Christ.

Each lesson includes a Scripture text, which the group will study together in the second third of the meeting, using the six interactive questions. The group leader should select a memory verse for each lesson, which will be memorized together during the final third of the meeting. In keeping with the pattern that has already been established, participants will review the summarized lesson so that they will be able to teach it to 3-5 people before the next meeting.

Each of the *Ten Stages of Spiritual Growth* contains two Bible lessons. These typically require five months of weekly meetings to complete. After these 20 lessons are completed, many house churches go on to study the gospel of Mark section by section. This is usually followed by studies of Acts and Ephesians.

The **first** stage, *Identification with the Death of Jesus Christ*, covers the lessons: The Lord's Supper (Matthew 26:26-35) and Facing Persecution (Acts 4:13-31).

The **second** stage, *New Birth*, covers the lessons: New Birth by the Holy Spirit (John 3:1-18) and Paul's Testimony (Acts 9:1-22).

The **third** stage, *New Family* (The Body of Christ), covers the lessons: The Head of the Body (Obedience to Christ, Matthew 4:18-25) and The Functions of the Body (the Church, Acts 2:29-47). It is at this point that the disciples covenant together to become a church.

The **fourth** stage, *Communicating with God* (Prayer), covers the lessons: Building Intimacy with God through the Lord's Prayer (Matthew 6:5-15) and Building Intimacy with God through Spontaneous Prayer (Matthew 7:7-11).

The **fifth** stage, *Spiritual Food* (The Word of God), covers the lessons: Building a Close Relationship with God through His Word (Luke 24:36-45) and Meeting with God (Luke 10:38-42).

The **sixth** stage, *New Clothes for Jesus' Followers*, covers the lessons: The Outer Garments (Ephesians 4:17-32) and The Inner Garments (Matthew 6:25-34).

The **seventh** stage, *Standing Firm*, covers two lessons: Overcoming Temptation (Matthew 4:1-11) and The Armor of God (Ephesians 6:10-18).

The **eighth** stage, *Walking as a Follower of Jesus*, covers two lessons: Walking in Faith (Matthew 14:22-33) and Walking in Surrender (John 13:13-17).

The **ninth** stage, *The Believer's Personality Traits*, covers two lessons: Love (Luke 10:30-37) and Hope (John 11:1-44).

The **tenth** stage, *Growing toward Maturity*, covers two lessons: Learning to Give (Mark 12:41-44) and Giving Birth to a New Church (Acts 16:6-15).

Equip Leaders

The final letter in our **ABIDE** acronym, and the final task to pursue in follow-up for a church-planting movement is equipping leaders. As multiple house churches develop, you will need to provide ongoing, on-the-job training for multiplying house church leaders and the leaders of the growing network of house churches. Try to do this informally and as locally as possible. Providing biblical, simple and reproducible leadership training materials is essential for church and church network leaders to grow strong and deep in the faith.

As the need arose, we developed a series of lessons that covered basic Christian doctrine, discipleship and leadership development (*Foundations*), as well as a systematic study through the entire New Testament (*Deep Roots*). House church network leaders meet weekly for local leadership training. These emerging leaders also meet monthly for accountability and to study the leadership training material. Good material addressing these matters is widely available, and so we will not provide it for you here.

No matter what material you choose to use to equip leaders, focus on the process as well as the material. Leadership training meetings should follow the same three-part format on which you patterned the follow-up sessions and house church formation.

Those who study the lessons must be able to teach them to believers in their house churches and networks. This is the 2 Timothy 2:2 principle at work: "And the things you have heard me say in the presence of many witnesses entrust to reliable men who will also be qualified to teach others." If you, instead, outsource leadership training to outsiders, non-local experts with advanced degrees, your leadership multiplication will break down, resulting in a shortage of leaders.

A VISUAL IMAGE OF THE ABIDE PLAN

From the beginning of the Any-3 process through follow-up, church formation, and leadership development, you have now been exposed to a lot of content. Many of our trainees have found it beneficial to see how all of this fits together, in a single visual image.

We have attempted to give you a one-page image of the Any-3 process from start to finish with a graphic that we call *The Big One*. *The Big One* displays the entire plan at a glance.

As your eyes trace this graphic from the bottom to the top, you will see each of the themes and elements that you have studied in this book. Spend time reviewing each of the five component parts of *The Big One*. Try to commit it to memory. Now take out a blank piece of paper and see if you can reproduce it for yourself. As you commit this single image to heart, it will help guide you in the various parts of Any-3, and how they can fit together to foster a church multiplication movement.

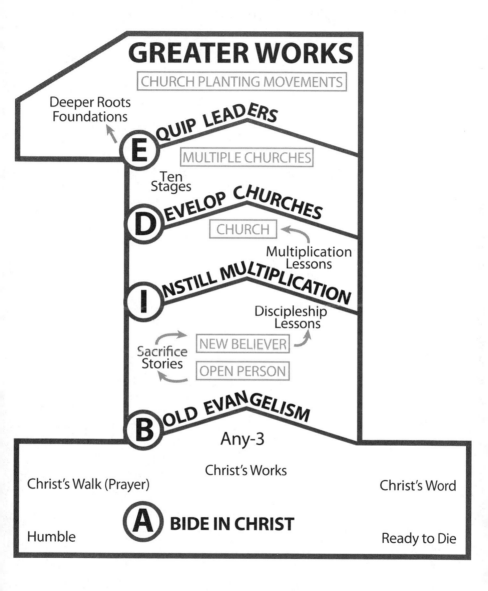

15
Launch!

AS THIS BOOK goes to print, we continually get new reports of how God is using Any-3 to stimulate effective evangelism in other corners of the Muslim world. God is using Any 3 to equip Christians with a bold new tool for harvesting where the Holy Spirit is at work. Some Muslim peoples are seeing their first converts in history, while others are already getting to multiplying generations of believers and churches.

OVERHEARD BY ANY-3 PRACTITIONERS

Any-3 evangelism often provokes memorable responses. Below are a few of the comments that have been uttered as Muslims are hearing the gospel through Any-3.

1) Anwar heard the gospel from a missionary doing an Any-3 workshop practicum and concluded, "God sent you here so I could hear this message."

2) A taxi driver named Isa heard the gospel through Any-3 and replied, "I have a friend who's already been talking to me about Jesus. What is the next step?"

3) A mission volunteer named Jesse was sharing the gospel through his translator when the Muslim man with whom

they were witnessing responded, "Last night I had a dream that two people came to my house with a message. One spoke the local language and the other did not. Could you be the persons I saw in my dream?"

4) Upon hearing the gospel, a hotel employee responded, "Actually, I like Jesus' teachings better than the teachings of our prophet."

5) During an Any-3 workshop, Joan and Helen shared the gospel with a Muslim woman named Leila who concluded, "God sent you here so I could hear this message."

6) An Arab Christian living in the Middle East learned Any-3 and immediately responded, "Now I have a clear and simple way to share the gospel with my Muslim neighbors."

7) Several times people have welcomed the Any-3 witness with the comment, "I recently saw the *Jesus Film* on television." This led to an easy discussion of Jesus' sacrifice for us on the cross.

8) Many people respond, "It appears that all roads do not lead to heaven. I can see now that there is only one way."

9) A mission volunteer named Bert was astounded when the Muslim man with whom he shared said, "Yes, it's true. The followers of Jesus know their sins are forgiven, but we Muslims don't have that assurance."

10) In a recent Any-3 evangelism push into a conservative Muslim province, nearly 25% of those who heard the gospel said "Yes" to Jesus, and prayed to invite him into their lives.

Any-3 is not a magical formula, but it is a reliable pathway to a clear and effective gospel presentation. The power is in the gospel -- Any-3 just multiplies gospel witness. Perhaps you've already noticed that Any-3's five-step process addresses common human concerns that are not really limited to the Muslim world.

As a result, many Christians have asked, "Could Any-3 be used to reach other, non-Muslim, groups?" The answer is, "Yes." This is already happening. Though some aspects of Any-3 will always need to be adapted to their target audience, the fundamental steps of Any-3 can apply to any lost people groups.

ANY-3 FOR EVERYONE

Because the gospel is for everyone, Any-3 is providing an effective pathway for sharing the gospel with Hindus, Buddhists, and nominal Christians as well. Minor adjustments to the approach and terminology make Any-3 culturally appropriate for each of these communities.

The basic aspects of Any-3 do not change. The characteristics of the witnessing encounter are similar: Intentional, Informal, Interactive, Initiative and Introducing the Messiah.

The five-step journey also remains unchanged: Get Connected, Get to a God Conversation, Get to Lostness, Get to the Gospel, and Get to a Decision.

The following paragraphs will offer some suggested adaptations to get you started using Any-3 with other religious communities.

Nominal Christians

Nominal Christians are persons who may call themselves Christians, whether Catholic, Protestant or Orthodox, who have not yet surrendered themselves to Christ through faith to receive God's forgiveness of their sins. They are still depending upon their works to save them, instead of Christ's sacrifice alone.

Recently a colleague trained some young seminary students in Any-3. Before doing the actual assignment of witnessing to lost people, one student tried out the approach on a local pastor. When asked what he was doing to get his sins forgiven, the pastor listed several good works that he hoped would save him. After admitting that he did not know for certain if he was saved, the pastor listened to the gospel then professed his faith in Christ alone. Indeed the gospel is different from religious works, even *Christian* religious works.

Witnessing to nominal Christians, especially Catholics and Orthodox, is not unlike witnessing to Muslims. The witnessing approach focuses on the doctrine of justification with the question, "What are you doing to pay off your sin debt to God?" Although the specific list of good deeds that Catholics and Orthodox must do to be justified according to their religious tenets is different from the requirements of Islam, both have well-defined religious rituals.

Getting connected is the same in every context. Getting to the point would still be done with the transition question, "Are you Hindu, Muslim, Buddhist or Christian?" This would be immediately followed by a discussion about our sinfulness, until we have common agreement that we are all sinners.

Just as in the Any-3 approach with Muslims, the witness would ask, "What are you doing to get your sins forgiven?" Using interactive questions, the witness would discuss the deeds, which they are doing to gain salvation. Close this section by using the standard three questions, "Are your sins forgiven yet? When will they be forgiven? Will they be forgiven on judgment day?"

Follow these transition questions with *The First and Last Sacrifice Story* and then transition into the final step of Any-3 *Getting to a Decision.*

Hindus

Though Hinduism has many variations, a common theme is the need to make offerings or acts of worship (called *puja*) to placate the anger of the spirit world. Hindus continually practice their religion through worship and sacrifice to prevent the gods from being angry with them.

When speaking to Hindus we focus on the doctrine of propitiation, rather than justification, as the bridge to establishing lostness. Propitiation means "the satisfaction of God's wrath." In other words, Jesus satisfied God's wrath toward sinners with his sacrificial atonement.

In *getting to lostness,* we can cite Romans 2, "But because of your stubbornness and unrepentant heart you are storing up wrath for yourself in the day of wrath and revelation of the righteous judgment of God, who will render to every man according to his deeds" (Romans 2:5-6).

We can ask our Hindu friend, "What are you doing so that the gods or spirits will not be angry with you?" After discussing the matter, the three follow-up questions would be: "Are the gods still angry with you?" "When will you reach the point where the gods are no longer angry with you?" and "When you die, will the gods still be angry with you? Once again, their efforts are not measuring up to reach the goal for which they seek, freedom from God's wrath, a freedom provided by the saving work of Jesus Christ.

The good news for Hindus is that, in Christ, God is no longer angry toward sinners. As Paul wrote, "For God has not destined us for wrath, but for obtaining salvation through our Lord Jesus Christ, who died for us...." (1 Thessalonians 5:9-10a).

We can then transition into *The First and Last Sacrifice Story* by saying, "What I believe is different. I know that God is not angry with me. God Himself made a way for His anger to be appeased." You can then follow the *First and Last Sacrifice Story* with the final step of Any-3 *Getting to a Decision.*[28]

Buddhists

Many folk Buddhists share a worldview that is similar to Hindus. Like Hindus, these folk Buddhists seek protection as

---

[28] Many missionaries who are using Any-3 with Hindus and Buddhists are substituting the *Creation to Christ* (C2C) story for *The First and Last Sacrifice Story. Creation to Christ* begins with the creation of the spirit world and continues chronologically through Christ's sacrifice and resurrection. If you choose to use *The First and Last Sacrifice Story,* consider adding a prelude establishing God's preexistence, and His creation of the spirit world, along with their fall into rebellion. This "fall of the spirit world" is also proving useful in helping Animistic people understand the nature of God's salvation.

well as blessing from the spirit world. In these instances, an approach similar to the Hindu adaptation of Any-3 is effective.

Some other schools of Buddhism seek to acquire merit that will allow them to break the cycle of reincarnation. Any-3 can engage this worldview with the question, "What are you doing to accumulate merit to break free from reincarnation?"

For many Buddhists, though, an emphasis on reconciliation with God speaks to their heart. Reconciliation is the doctrine that through Christ's atonement on the cross, He restored peace with God. Stated differently, we are no longer God's enemies.

People are all trying to do the right things, so they can have peace with God. The problem is that we never quite achieve total peace with God. Each day we commit sins, which reminds us that we are separated from God.

The apostle Paul presented the doctrine of reconciliation in his letter to the Corinthians, "Now all *these* things are from God, who reconciled us to Himself through Christ, and gave us the ministry of reconciliation, namely, that God was in Christ reconciling the world to Himself, not counting their trespasses against them, and He has committed to us the word of reconciliation" (2 Corinthians 5:18-19).

Practicing Any-3 with Buddhists, we might *get to lostness* by asking, "What are you doing to gain peace with God?" The section would end by asking them, "Are you certain that you are at peace with God?" "When will that happen?" "When you die, will you achieve the oneness and peace with God that you desire?"

As usual, the witness can transition to the gospel by saying, "What I believe is different." Follow this with, "I know I am at peace with God, but not just because I try to be a good person. I am at peace with God because God Himself has already made peace with mankind."

Because Adam and Eve disobeyed God's command and ate from the tree of the knowledge of good and evil, they were alienated from God; their relationship with God was broken. They could no longer enjoy the walks and talks within the garden with their loving God. Instead, they chose to keep their sin hidden. God wanted to be reconciled to the man and woman He created, so He called out to them, "Where are you?" God desires a reconciled relationship with His creation.

Then, you can share a gospel presentation such as *The First and Last Sacrifice Story*. Though Buddhists generally abhor the idea of blood sacrifice, it does underscore the great price paid for our sins, and for our reconciliation. As we speak of Christ's self-sacrifice, we can emphasize His words: "It is finished." Christ is the last sacrifice. And for a Buddhist, that truly is good news.

Whatever people group or worldview you are trying to reach, the five steps of Any-3 can provide you with a trustworthy and biblical path from Connection to Christ. Just as the gospel penetrated the pluralistic worldviews of Jesus' day, so too, can it speak to men and women today.

"GO TO HEAVEN!"

Jesus gave his Great Commission sermon at least five times during five different post-resurrection appearances. Each time he emphasized something different. In Matthew 28:18-20, Jesus spoke of the discipleship process -- going, baptizing, and teaching. In Mark 16:15-16 and Acts 1:8, He emphasized its magnanimous scope: The gospel is for everyone, and baptism is for every believer. In Luke 24:44-47, Jesus presented the message of the crucified and risen Messiah.

John's report of Jesus' Great Commission particularly challenges us. "So Jesus said to them again, 'Peace be with you, as the Father has sent Me, I also send you.' And when He had said this, He breathed on them and said to them, 'Receive the Holy Spirit.'" Jesus' disciples were to be His feet and His voice to proclaim His salvation. The Holy Spirit would precede them, fill them, and work alongside them.

The next words from Jesus astound us still today. Jesus said, "If you forgive the sins of any, they have been forgiven them;

if you retain the sins of any, they have been retained'" (John 20:23). Jesus was saying, "Forgiveness of sins is in *your* hands." As Christ's disciples, when we choose to share the gospel, or not, we are choosing to offer forgiveness or or not. To be clear, forgiveness was purchased by God and is received when a lost soul says "yes" to Jesus (John 3:18, 36), but it is to us alone, the gospel bearers, that Christ has given both the authority and the responsibility to proclaim that offer of forgiveness.

Stated more bluntly, withholding the gospel is saying to someone, "Go to Hell!" Sharing the gospel is saying, "Believe in Christ's sacrifice, and your sins will be forgiven! So, believe, and go to heaven!"

Paul understood the gravity of this responsibility. At the end of his ministry in Ephesus, he was able to say:

> ...*I consider my life worth nothing to me, if only I may finish the race and complete the task the Lord Jesus has given me—the task of testifying to the gospel of God's grace. Now I know that none of you among whom I have gone about preaching the kingdom will ever see me again. Therefore, I declare to you today that I am innocent of the blood of all men. (Acts 20:24-26)*

Paul departed his ministry in Ephesus with a clear conscience, because he had testified to the gospel (v. 24). This should be the aim of every minister of the gospel.

In our Asian country, an elderly woman named Fatima was plagued by fear of her impending death. Then one day, a volunteer using Any-3 shared the gospel with Fatima. Fatima had never heard it before, but it was what she had been searching for. Fatima believed the message and immediately received Christ. Fatima began clapping her hands and saying, "I'm ready to go now."

CHALLENGE AND LAUNCH

This good news of forgiveness in Christ is "the faith which was once for all delivered to the saints" (Jude 3b), "...for it is the power of God for salvation to everyone who believes" (Romans 1:16). This gospel power that flowed through the early Church is the only reason that Any-3 is effective today. Ordained by God, purchased by Christ and activated by the Holy Spirit, the simple, timeless good news presented through Any-3 can be unleashed in your own ministry.

The principles and patterns of Any-3 are not new, yet always new. Modeled and mandated by Christ twenty centuries ago, it is a method and message that still speaks today to anyone, anywhere, and anytime.

Appendices

APPENDIX A
Old Testament Sacrifice Follow-up Stories[29]

Cain and Abel Story

After they were banished from Paradise, Adam and Eve had two sons, Cain and Abel. Cain became a farmer, while Abel became a shepherd. One day both brought sacrifices to God – Cain from his field, but Abel sacrificed an animal from his flock. God accepted Abel's sacrifice, but not Cain's. Cain became jealous of his brother. Although God warned Cain to repent, he killed Abel instead. God punished Cain. Abel, by contrast, was justified and inherited eternal life (Hebrews 11:4).[30]

Noah Story

The world became full of evil. Only Noah was considered by God to be a righteous man. Therefore, God decided to destroy

---

[29] In the first follow-up visit we retell the Adam and Eve portion of *The First and Last Sacrifice Story* again, and add the Cain and Abel story to it to form one story. It is helpful to retell the Adam and Eve story during the first follow-up visit because it becomes the foundation for moving forward with open persons, once they profess faith, to use Any-3.

[30] The point to emphasize in the Cain and Abel story is that God accepted the blood sacrifice, but rejected other sacrifices of our choosing.

the world with a flood. Only Noah, his family, and some from each kind of animal would be saved.

By faith Noah built a boat in obedience to God's command, although it had never before rained on the earth. God warned Noah and his family to get into the Ark along with the animals, and then God shut the door. For forty days and nights a flood covered the entire earth, but God protected Noah's family in the ark. However, all of the people and animals that hadn't entered the Ark were destroyed.

When the floodwater subsided, the ark came to land on Mt. Ararat. At that time Noah built an altar and offered a sacrifice from the animals on the Ark. Although Noah and his family were spared from temporary judgment by entering the Ark, they still needed a substitute for their sin.[31] When God smelled the aroma of the sacrifice, He promised that he would never again destroy every living thing on the earth, as He had done with the flood. God gave a rainbow as a sign that He would never destroy the entire earth with a flood again.

Abraham Story

Abraham lived his life in faith and obedience. God promised Abraham that he would be the father of many nations (Genesis 17:4). But Abraham and his wife Sarah became old and were yet to have children. Even so, God once again promised Abraham a son through his wife, Sarah.

Even though at times Abraham's faith wavered, God gave him and his wife a son late in life. And then several years later, unexpectedly, God told Abraham to sacrifice his son! Believing that God would provide a sacrifice, Abraham offered his son in obedience to what he was told. However, when he was just at the point of killing his son, the angel of the LORD stopped

---

[31] The point to emphasize is that even though Noah and his family were safe from temporary disaster because they entered the ark, they still offered animal sacrifices to atone for their sin debt.

him. God provided a ram for a sacrifice. Only God can provide a suitable sacrifice.[32]

Moses Story: Passover

The descendants of Jacob, Abraham's grandson, settled in Egypt. They were enslaved by the Egyptians as their numbers increased. God sent Moses to Pharaoh, king of Egypt, to demand their freedom. Each time Pharaoh rejected God's demands, He sent disasters as punishments upon Egypt. This happened ten times.

The final punishment was for God to kill all of the firstborn sons and firstborn cattle throughout the land. There was only one way to avoid this calamity.

Only those who obeyed God's requirement would be saved. God commanded Abraham's children to sacrifice an unblemished lamb, and put its blood on their doorposts and lintel of their door.

There was weeping throughout the land of Egypt as the firstborn sons and cattle of each family died. God mercifully passed over those who had sacrificed a lamb, and they were saved. With this final punishment, Pharaoh allowed the people to go free from Egypt.[33]

Moses Story: Law

After delivering Abraham's descendants from slavery in Egypt, God summoned Moses to the top of Mt. Sinai. There He gave Moses the Law. The Law included ten primary commandments, along with hundreds of other commandments based on these ten commandments.

The purpose of the law was for God's people to live holy lives, because God is holy. People often broke the Commandments,

---

[32] The point to emphasize in the Abraham story is that God both required a living sacrifice, and then provided that sacrifice.

[33] The obvious point of the Passover story is that the lamb's blood atoned for the sins of the people.

rather than obeying them. Judgment always resulted from disobedience to God's commandments.

What were people to do for forgiveness when they broke God's laws? The Law itself stated that blood sacrifices were the price for sins to be forgiven. A person must bring an unblemished sacrificial animal, and place his hand on the animal's head, showing that the person's sin was being transferred to the animal. The animal was then killed, demonstrating that the wages of sin is death. The priest would then sprinkle some of the animal's blood on the altar, and the person's sin would be atoned for. Only God can determine how sins are atoned, and He instituted blood sacrifice as the way of atonement.[34]

---

[34] The point to emphasize in this story is that the Law of God prescribes blood sacrifice as necessary for the atonement for sin.

Illustrations for Any-3

Here are a few brief illustrations to put in your toolbox to help clarify some points of Any-3.

Human Effort Cannot Forgive Sins

It is helpful in the Any-3 process to explain that people often try to become holy by doing good works, but they never make it all the way to God. They are continually failing. To illustrate, I raise one hand to eye height. I explain that God is holy, and we try to become holy like God. I put my other hand around waist height, showing that we often do good works, or attempt worship practices to become holy and we succeed for a while, but then we fall down again. "We climb, then fall; climb, then fall. We never even come close to making it to the top. We are frustrated because our religious effort is never enough to forgive our sins."

Sin is Like a Debt

When we ask the person, "When will your sins be forgiven?" in the 'Get to Lostness' section, we sometimes use the following illustration.

"Our sin is like a debt. Each time we sin, our debt grows larger. When we have borrowed money, we more or less know how much we owe and when it will be paid off. In the same way, we try to pay off our sin debt with our good deeds. If you keep paying at the rate you are paying now, when will your sins be forgiven?"

By the way, the person rarely gives an answer, but he admits that he does not know when his sins will be paid off.

Motorcycle Illustration

When doing Any-3, we sometimes hear people say, "I think God will forgive my sins, because He is merciful." Even after hearing *The First and Last Sacrifice Story*, occasionally they still respond this way. Sometimes, God has used the following illustration to get the conversation back on track.

"Suppose a person wants to buy a motorcycle.[35] He usually makes a payment plan at the bank to pay X amount each month. Let us say I bought a motorcycle this way, but when it was time to pay the first month's payment, I did not have enough money. So I tried to find a way out of this mess. I gathered five chickens that I was raising to feed my family, and took the chickens to the bank. Imagine walking into the bank with chickens. People are looking at you like you are weird, and you are embarrassed. Finally, the cashier calls your number, so you approach the counter with your chickens and lay them on the counter. Will the bank accept your chickens as payment for the motorcycle? Of course not, the banker will laugh, right? Why? Because the agreement for payment was money, not chickens. That is how it is with God. God has made an agreement with mankind that sin can only be paid for through the shedding of blood. And Jesus shed His blood as the final and only way for people's sins to be forgiven."

---

[35] Motorcycles are the most common vehicle in my country. Adapt the illustration to your own setting substituting car, truck, bicycle or whatever connects with your community.

No Proud People In Heaven

When witnessing to Muslims, two scenarios often occur. Sometimes they propose that if we could know that our sins were already forgiven, then we would commit sin intentionally after conversion. Also, they might persist in insisting that they will enter heaven because of their good works. In either scenario, the following illustration has proven helpful. It affirms the principle of Romans 4:2, that if we could be justified by our works that we would become proud of our own accomplishment rather than Christ's work on our behalf.

Let's suppose that I'm a good person, and I entered heaven because of my works. I'd probably be proud, wouldn't you? That's how people are. When we succeed because of our capabilities, we become proud and boast about it. However, there are no proud people in heaven, are there? Actually, there is only one person in heaven who can be proud, and that is God, because He made a way for our sins to be forgiven. In heaven, those who have received Jesus will be humble, because we realize that we're there because of Christ's sacrifice, not because of our good works.

Pork Illustration[36]

An illustration some Any-3 practitioners have used effectively with Muslims is the Pork Illustration. The point of the illustration is that all people are sinners, and no matter how great or small their sins, all of us are separated from God. The illustration is as follows:

Both the Mosaic and Islamic Laws forbid the eating of pork. Let us suppose that I offer to you a bowl of cooked pork. Are you allowed to eat it or not? A Muslim will naturally respond, "No, I am not permitted to eat it."

"Suppose I only place a small piece of pork in a bowl. Then I cover it up with rice and vegetables so that it is no longer visible.

---

[36] This illustration came from a colleague who is leading another movement of Muslims to Christ.

Are you permitted to eat the contents of that bowl?" A Muslim will correctly answer that he must not eat the contents of that bowl either. Then ask, "Which bowl of food will you choose to eat?" The hearer may wrestle with the idea but will conclude that neither bowl of food containing pork may be eaten.

At this point the witness presents the scenario of two sinners, one with obvious sins like murder and adultery, and another with hidden, less-obvious sins. Which person will God welcome into heaven upon his death? The answer is that neither will be received, because they are both sinners and God is holy.